GANGSTER HOLIDAYS

GANGSTER HOLIDAYS
The Lore and Legends
of the Bad Guys

TOM HOLLATZ

NORTH STAR PRESS OF ST. CLOUD, INC.

Cover design: Corinne A. Dwyer

Copyright © 1989 Tom Hollatz

Second Printing: December 1989

Printed in the United States of
America by Park Press, Inc.,
Waite Park, Minnesota.

Published by:
**North Star Press of
St. Cloud, Inc.**
P.O. Box 451
St. Cloud, Minnesota 56302

ISBN: 0-87839-053-7

Dedication

For:
Jim Ford, Bill Granger, Bill Trible
Emil Wanatka Jr.
and
Chester Gould/Dick Tracy

CONTENTS

PREFACE

In November of 1924, Professor Frederick M. Thrasher of the University of Chicago stated, after a three-year study, that 100,000 gangsters lived in Chicago. Professor Thrasher's investigation reported the existence of 1,313 gangs of safe blowers, porch climbers, professional gunmen, labor agitators, and "specialists of every kind in the category of crime."

Chicago was labeled by the nation's press as the "crime cradle" of the world.

Prohibition began January 17, 1920 and was finally ended on December 5, 1933. The Roaring '20s and the Heated '30s, triggered by Prohibition, mixed a crime brew whose hangover lingers today.

In this era anti-heroes seemed to be glorified by the newspapers which were paying one dollar a word to get copy on the likes of Al Capone. It was a time linked to the anti-heroes of the late nineteenth century who were also idolized by the press and the pulp novels of the day—Calamity Jane, Belle Starr, the Daltons, Jesse and Frank James, Al Jennings, Judge Roy Bean, the Clantons and Billy the Kid.

Even the "good guys" of this time were wild, flamboyant and colorful—"Wild Bill" Hickock, William B. "Bat" Masterson and Wyatt Berry Stapp Earp. They rivaled the law enforcers of the '20s and '30s like Edgar Hoover, Melvin Purvis and Elliot Ness.

It is not surprising, then, that the so-called "heroes" of this later period were still influenced by the Wild West era both in names and character—John Dillinger, Baby Face Nelson, Al Capone and Ralph Capone, Bonnie and Clyde, the Barkers, Pretty Boy Floyd, Machine Gun Kelly. These were the rogues of the day.

The era also featured some dramatic exclamation points:

February 14, 1929—The St. Valentine's Day Massacre. Seven lieutenants of the Bugs Moran gang were slaughtered in a Chicago warehouse.

October 24, 1929— Black Thursday on Wall Street. The jolt could not have come at a worse time for the United States and its 122 million who were still shaking from the Flapper era. The press daily carried accounts of people losing everything as many blue chip securities fell 50 percent. The losses on paper totaled $26 billion.

Conditions everywhere grew increasingly bleak. Agnes Meyer, wife of Eugene Meyer, head of the United States Federal Reserve Board, described man's universal plight in the early 1930s: "The world is literally rocking beneath our feet."

Europe's social and economic upheavals spawned rising totalitarianisms—Hitler and Mussolini.

In 1933, the Chicago World's Fair, the Century of Progress Exposition, opened in the face of that worldwide depression. It seemed bizarre, and yet a much-needed shot-in-the-arm at the same time.

John Dillinger and his seemingly miraculous escapes and escapades sparked a fascination with Public Enemy No. 1 that continues to this day.

Children as well as their parents could name the top crooks and the top baseball batting averages in a single breath.

Chicago, the "crime cradle" of the headlines, has cold-damp winters and hot-steamy summers. With the lake at its back and only 600 feet above sea level, the dampness and humidity can be oppressive. The Northwoods of Wisconsin, however, are 1,600 feet plus above sea level and have "dry" winters and naturally air-conditioned summers.

Early ads of the Chicago & Northwestern Railways lured the rich Chicagoans north with the promise of that natural coolness and summer vacations in the lakes region of the Northwoods. That same ad also said: "Ideal location for summer homes."

It's not surprising that the gangsters, too, enjoyed escaping the city's heat (police included) to vacation in the woods. Like other wealthy Chicago tourists, the hoods hunted, fished, swam and otherwise enjoyed themselves in the relaxed vacation atmosphere with family and friends.

In the city, the war between the good guys and the bad guys could never be forgotten. Neither could let themselves forget the danger. At any time, without any warning, a .45 slug from a Thompson submachine gun could splatter their brains on the pavement.

In the woods, all seemed different.

Antoinette Giancana recalled in her book *Mafia Princess* that the family vacation in the Rhinelander area with daddy Sam was one of her fondest memories of her green years. All seemed wonderful in her life for one magic summer in the Northwoods.

The gangsters who ventured north are still remembered with an awe and a reverence by many of the old timers. "Yeah, that Ralph Capone was a marvelous human being" could be an accolade used by the locals to describe any of the gangsters who ventured there, or so it seems.

They were there—and many still come—to drink of that peaceful brew that the Northwoods wilds offer.

Introduction

I've always enjoyed my trips to Manitowish Waters in the wilds of Wisconsin's Northwoods and those special dinners at Little Bohemia, the scene of the famed John Dillinger shootout on April 22, 1934.

Entering the quaint restaurant is an instant step into another era—the '30s. Bullet holes in the windows are strange reminders of that violent night in 1934 when Dillinger, America's Public Enemy No. 1, Baby Face Nelson, and his gang eluded an attack by a confused FBI contingent and several local law enforcement agents.

There is a haunting fascination with those gangsters of the 1920s and 1930s. As one old timer in Mercer, Wisconsin, once told me, the mobsters of that era were considered to be Robin Hoods of sorts.

"They didn't shoot your ma or pa. What they did was gun down those no good sons-of-bitches, the bankers, who were stealing their homes and farms during the Depression. They were lashing back at the system that suddenly went crazy. Good hard-working people were out on their rears in the cold. The gangsters fought back with bullets as they grabbed loot from the banks . . ."

After ten more brews, it began to make sense in a strange way.

It was in Mercer where the locals would not say a cruel word about Ralph "Bottles" Capone, who moved there in 1942. Ralph, I was told, helped out many who were about to lose their homes. Ralph, too, loved to participate in local events.

Not only did Ralph Capone and Dillinger vacation or hide out in the Northwoods, but others like "Scarface" himself, Al Capone, had a magnificent estate in Couderay, Wisconsin, which is a tourist attraction today. The home is as it was in 1925.

Fleeing the violent Depression shootouts and the turf wars on Chicago's Prohibition front, the gangsters headed North to taste the peace and quiet offered in that beautiful part of the Earth.

The Northwoods is a beautiful area. It has more lakes in one concentrated area than anywhere on the planet. The woods, too, are a magnet for the city folk, who usually visit once and are hooked for life.

A friend and former colleague of mine at the Chicago *Tribune* once visited me here at Bear Lodge in Boulder Junction, Wisconsin, and couldn't believe the natural beauty. After that first visit to the Northwoods, he told me, "I've always wanted to retire in Key West. Now I know where I'm going to retire . . . in the Northwoods."

No wonder the gangsters were drawn here. The woods do strange things to people. When you mix in equal doses, the eldritch sounds of the Common Loon, the Northern lights, crisp summer nights, bright warm days and the high azure blue skies, the recipe is something that settles in one's soul.

Tom Hollatz
Trout Lake House
10699 North Creek Road
Boulder Junction,
Wisconsin 54512

GANGSTER HOLIDAYS

THE ERA

Prohibition

On January 17, 1920, the Volstead Act became law. This law, quite simply, made it illegal to make, transport, purchase and consume alcohol. Alcohol was bad, right? People became drunks, wasting hard-earned money that should have gone into their babies' mouths, right? Everyone should be glad that one evil had been removed from American society, right? Wrong. Prohibition wasn't necessarily a bad idea, but it was an exceedingly unpopular one. Beer and booze were too much a part of the American way of life, the economy and tradition to be wiped out by a law. For every temperance leaguer, there were a dozen drinkers—not drunks or bums living on the streets—but good law-abiding, productive citizens who liked the taste and high of alcohol, and had a few bucks to spend getting some.

But how did a respectable business man get his clean hands on a product that was illegal? Enter the bootlegger. Enter the moonshiner and brewer. And where could an "honest" citizen go to sip this illegal substance? Ice cream parlors, restaurants, road houses and pop palaces took on new life as speakeasies. For every means the government devised to control the flow of alcohol, the creative minds of the criminal element came up with a dozen ways to outwit, confuse, get around and otherwise foil the righteous enforcers from upholding the law.

In an effort to keep a nation dry that really didn't want to stay dry, the government spent some $363,000,000.00 in the fourteen years the Volstead Act was law, trying to enforce that unenforceable law. At the same time, state and local governments spent some three billion dollars mopping up the wetness. Neither got its money's worth; the booze kept flowing.

In 1931, after a two-year study, the Wickersham Commission told President Hoover that it would cost the American taxpayers $10,000,000.00 a day to continue the effort to keep the nation dry. But by then, other factors made it all but impossible to sustain the effort.

The Great Depression

Beginning with the stock market crash on October 24, 1929, and lasting throughout the 1930s, the Great Depression was felt all the way up to World War II when the gearing up for war began to put people back to work, build up the economy and ease the nation away from the dreary lives of the Depression.

The nation was already four years into the Depression by the time the Wickersham Commission brought its results to President Hoover. The verdict was clear: when the nation was suffering so badly on all fronts, the government just could not afford to spend its money fighting the losing battle of dryness. On December 5, 1933, the end came to Prohibition by way of the 21st Amendment to the Constitution.

The Depression had other effects on the time, however. People were losing their homes, farms and businesses because they could not make a go of it any more. Drought hit the Midwest with a vengeance. Foreclosures were as much a part of life as death and taxes. Almost every facet of society from the wealthiest who took a thumping in the Stock Market Crash to the poor who discovered they could be even poorer—everyone experienced hardship and privation. It was the first time cinching up one's belt was just not enough to solve the problems society had to face. Nothing seemed to be working. People looked for ways to sustain themselves. After food and shelter, they looked to brighten their depressed lives. Enter the anti-hero. In a way it's amazing that people like John Dillinger and Al Capone could be looked at as anything but the destructive, murderous, thieving men they were, but the 1920s and 1930s were times of turmoil and unfulfilled dreams. If a man saw nothing much wrong with a good stiff drink now and then, but the government said it was wrong, there was a tendency to look at the government as the cockeyed one. That made the bootlegger a kind of hero. If the land that had been settled and fought for was taken away by some bank, then the bank-robber became a modern day Robin Hood. It all followed a perverse logic a part of the times.

Always aware of a good publicity shot, FBI chief J. Edgar Hoover shows 1930s America's darling, Shirley Temple, a crime-detecting microscope in the FBI lab. In 1933 the old Bureau of Investigation (BI) became the U.S. Bureau of Investigation (USBI). It was in 1934 that it became the FBI (Federal Bureau of Investigation). *FBI Photo.*

During the Depression, entertainment was fairly hard to come by. Drinking and gambling were certainly right there at the top of the list of entertainment hits. There were no televisions yet and radio wasn't as much a part of the lives of people as it would become, but movies were very popular. And what did people like to see? Certainly not remakes of their difficult lives. They wanted to see bright lights, laughing children and gorgeous mansions where the rich (and their imaginations) played. The big gangsters, of course, lived that rich lifestyle out. The point was hard to miss.

Newspapers were more than news. On the front pages of the

newspapers of the day, huge headlines told of murder, gangsters, escapes and arrests. This was a large part of the entertainment for a lot of people. Following the bloody trails of criminals was a lot more fun than staring at the want ads and the job lists that didn't exist. The name of John Dillinger and Al Capone could get a tired heart to pumping and pass the idle minutes. It was worth the ink.

The Gun That Made the Roaring '20s Roar

The most interesting part of the television special "The Mystery of Al Capone's Vaults" was host Geraldo Rivera's test firing of a tommy gun in the Lexington Hotel. The savageness of those blazingly brutal bursts was only a tame taste of the way the gangsters tossed out hot lead at their rivals and police on the streets of Chicago.

The Saltis-McErlane gang, controllers of the Southwest Side of Chicago, introduced the tommy gun or the "Chicago Piano" into

Time magazine described the Thompson submachine gun as the deadliest weapon, pound for pound, ever devised by man. It will ever be known as the murder weapon that made the Roaring '20s roar! *Auto-Ordinance Corp. photo.*

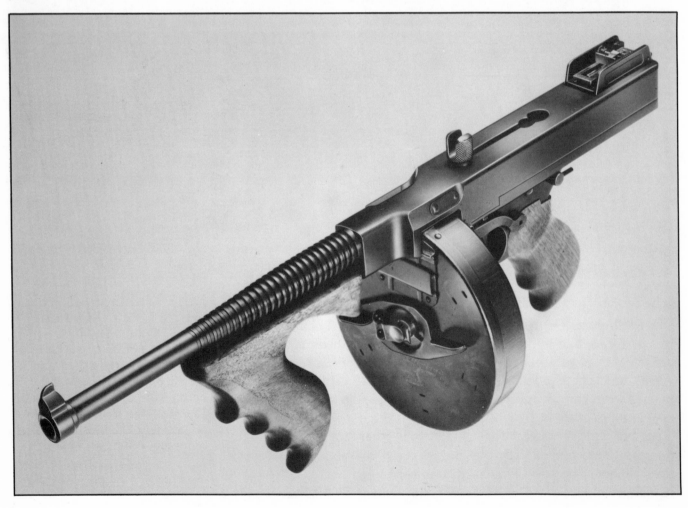

their violent world. A *Collier*'s reporter described the "chopper" or "typewriter" as "the greatest aid to bigger and better business the criminal has discovered in this generation . . . a diabolical machine of death . . . the highest-powered instrument of destruction that has been placed at the convenience of the criminal element . . . the diabolical acme of human ingenuity in man's effort to devise a mechanical contrivance with which to murder his neighbor."

The Thompson submachine gun was named after its inventor, Brig. Gen. John T. Thompson, director of arsenals during World War I. It was developed too late (1920) for use in the trenches, but Thompson still called it a "trench broom." The submachine gun was placed on the open market by Auto Ordinance Corporation of New York.

For the most part, the Thompson submachine gun was shunned by most military agencies in the United States and overseas. The reason seems to be that the weapon fit no traditional category.

J. Edgar Hoover was named the first head of the FBI on July 29, 1933. Here Hoover examines some of the weapons captured by his federal agents. Despite a rocky start as head of the new agency—especially when Dillinger escaped with his men from Little Bohemia—Hoover rebounded with the fire and tenacity of a pit bull. *FBI photo.*

Eliot Ness

Eliot Ness (1902-1957) headed the "Untouchables" (predecessors of today's ATF—Alcohol, Tobacco and Firearms—special agents). Based on evidence gathered by Ness and his raiders, Al Capone and 68 members of his gang were charged with conspiring to violate the Volstead Act. Five thousand separate offenses were cited, 4,000 of them consisting of beer truck deliveries. The income tax cases took precedence. *FBI photo.*

Law enforcement agencies ignored it too, claiming it could endanger innocent bystanders. Yet, the hoods, who seldom concerned themselves with such niceties, loved the gun, and saw it as the ultimate enforcement weapon.

The design of the tommy gun was as "clean" as its capabilities. It was light, weighing only 8.5 pounds. Yet it could fire up to a thousand .45-caliber pistol cartridges per minute. It also had an excellent range of 500 yards and could penetrate a pine board some three inches thick. Its rat-a-tat-tat fire power at close range was equally awesome. At close range it could cut down a tree trunk 23 inches in diameter. It worked like a drill on armor plating up to one-quarter inch thick. It was the hot knife the gangsters used on the butter of a heavy automobile. The 1923 Model A was equipped with a 20-cartridge box magazine.

The tommy gun could be had for $175.00 by mail order. Extra magazines cost just $3.00 apiece and the 50-cartridge unit was $21.

Most cities and states of the period enacted gun-control legislation similar to the 1911 New York Sullivan Law which sought to prohibit the possession of small, easily concealed firearms. Those laws placed no restrictions on the Thompson submachine gun. In order to purchase a Chicago Piano, all the purchaser needed to do was sign his name and give his address.

When the loopholes were tightened, the black market price for "clean" tommy guns went as high as $2,000.

What the Colt was to the West, the Thompson submachine gun was to the gangster era. It, quite literally, made the 1920s roar. It was the first weapon designed for automatic fire. It was devastating in its personality; it was accurate, easy to use and, when fired, it was controllable, with little or no rise. It was also comfortable to fire. And, just in case of a quick getaway, the stock could be removed to make it easier to fire out of speeding cars.

The tommy gun was the main speaker at the famed St. Valentine's Day Massacre; no one talked back.

Some historians claim the first use of the tommy gun came in the shooting of Jim Doherty and Tom Duffy, gunmen of the O'Donnell gang, and William H. McSwiggin, an assistant state's attorney. On April 27, 1926, in front of the Pony Inn in Cicero, Illinois, these men were gunned down in a hail of fire, most likely from the tommy gun. Other historians hold out for that dubious honor going to Joe Saltis and Frank McErland, leaders of the Southwest Side gang, who introduced the tommy gun to regain disputed territory claimed by the O'Donnell gang. They got their interests back.

The Cars

By the 1920s and 1930s, the auto had become an integral part of the crime world. No longer were the crooks escaping on horseback, but with horsepower. The Jesse James days were over for good. By the 1920s, cars were common enough that escaping criminals could readily find one to steal. Gas stations were proliferating. Roads were improving and being cut into the landscape all over the country. The vehicles themselves were advancing in size, weight, reliability and, most importantly, speed. The Ford in which Dillinger was said to have escaped the Feds at Little Bohemia, screamed away from the scene at 100 mph, not incredibly fast by today's standards, perhaps, but plenty fast for the era.

Automobiles offered some other advantages to the gangsters of the 1920s and 1930s that horses could not give them. Several men

Henry Ford received unsolicited testimonials for his cars from underworld "stars" Clyde Barrow and John Dillinger. Both men prized Fords for their getaway power.

Killers Bonnie and Clyde were gunned down May 23, 1934. They drove to the police ambush in a Ford. About a month before, Clyde Barrow had written Ford:

"While I still got breath in my lungs, I will tell you what a dandy car you make. I have driven Fords exclusively, when I could get away with one . . ."

Dillinger used two stolen Fords in his April 1934 getaway from Little Bohemia. He abandoned the first Ford—stained with blood—not far from St. Paul, Minnesota. There, he stole the second Ford.

In May, he wrote Henry Ford from Chicago (but had the letter mailed from Detroit as a false clue for police):

Hello Old Pal,

Arrived here at 10:00 a.m. today. Would like to drop in and see you.

You have a wonderful car. Been driving it for three weeks. It's a treat to drive one. Your slogan should be: 'Drive a Ford and watch the other cars fall behind you.' I can make any other car take a Ford's dust."

Bye-Bye.

John Dillinger

FBI photos.

could ride in a car at a time. That meant a number of things. One drove while others could hang out the windows with tommy guns, thus creating "drive by" hits on rivals. With one car, the whole bank-robbing team could escape together. Women, almost never taken along on previous "jobs" (unless they were active, gun-totting members of the gang) could now be settled comfortably in the back seat while the gang pulled a heist.

Cars also provided gangsters a certain amount of protection both during a job or getting from place to place. The cars could take

It wasn't only cars and trucks that came into action in the Prohibition years. This crew is making a "dry" run at Chicago's municipal airport preparing for the repeal of Prohibition. *Camera/100 Collection.*

a lot of lead and keep running; they could take a lot of lead meant for the gangsters inside. On a fast getaway, fleeing crooks could jump on the running boards until distance was put between them and the Feds or police. Cars could even be used as weapons. While a horse could kick or bite, an automobile could bowl someone over at top speed. Cars could also be used as battering rams (something a horse might just object to), breaking through police blockades, fences, even buildings if necessary. It's no wonder that crime proliferated during this time—the criminals could often afford bigger, better and faster cars than the police!

IN THE NORTHWOODS

Burlington, Wisconsin

Burlington, in southeastern Wisconsin, was watched as a barometer for gangsterism making its way into the state. The Milwaukee *Journal* sent a reporter to that resort community just to check out reports of gangster influence. This is part of the report:

> ... A visit to the hotels and resorts does not reveal to the ordinary observer the presence of any of the gangster element, although some may be present. That, however, is not remarkable, for the modern gangster is usually dapper and well dressed, and one might easily take a banker for a gangster and a gangster for a banker.

The gangsters did dress well and drove nice automobiles. Unless they had faces recognizable to the general public, the simple registering under a different name was enough to keep their underworld ties out of their way when having fun. It might also be true that many of the gangsters traveled just a bit north for their vacations, up to the Northwoods ... but not all of them ...

On November 2, 1929, Burlington was the site of a strange murder. The Associated Press reported it:

> The bullet-pierced body of an unidentified man, believed by authorities to have been the "passenger" of a gangland "ride," was found in a thicket on Mount Thom, a high hill south of [Burlington].
> The man, well dressed, about 35 and apparently of Italian extrac-

The quaint and beautiful island city of Minocqua, Wisconsin, in the heart of the "wilds" of the Northwoods. It was here that the 1930s gangsters—as well as a lot of other tourists—came for recreation. In nearby Woodruff, the gangsters would head for Ma Bailey's brothel operated by Margaret Bailey.

This aerial view of Minocqua was taken during hot-air balloon races. *Tom Hollatz photo.*

tion, had been shot eight times in the head and chest. The assassins stood so close that there were powder burns on the vest of his green suit.

A card and bill of sale in pockets of the man's clothing led officials to believe he was a Chicagoan . . . police found $33 in his pockets, and his expensive watch was still running.

Trixie's Private Funeral

Long before Ma Bailey's (now Joe Kelly's Landing), in Woodruff, Wisconsin, existed, the most famous whorehouse in the Northwoods was Trixie's, in Minocqua. Trixie's was on the west side of the present Highway 51 where B.J.'s Sport Shop now stands. This tale is told by aged Minocqua resident Al Ray:

Trixie was marvelous, or at least my father said she was. My dad went there frequently.

Trixie's was a class place, and well run. It's not the gents of the community who wanted the place to die, but their wives. When Trixie died, the do-gooders and the holy rollers of the community barred Trixie from being buried in the so-called "Christian" cemetery. This marvelous woman had given so much of herself to the community, and in the end she wasn't allowed to get down in the dirt with the girls, so to speak.

My dad took Trixie's body in his boat on Lake Minocqua and found her a permanent burial place. That place is just east of Jossart Island. He never told anyone on what part of the island he buried her as she was placed in the grave with all of her diamonds and jewels—which were considerable.

I miss Ma Bailey's [too]. She always called me "captain." Margaret (Ma) always wore a white nurse's uniform behind the bar. "Want a blonde tonight?" she'd say as I walked in. It was a class place.

Norwood Pines, Minocqua

Norwood Pines supper club is located just west of Minocqua, Wisconsin, south of Highway 70 on quaint Patricia Lake. The long driveway, through tall pines, takes the visitor back to a time when gambling was one of the main pleasures in the wilds of the Wisconsin Northwoods.

When Frank Tillman built Norwood Pines in 1939, prostitution was also in vogue in this rustic setting. Upstairs was a pleasure heaven known as the northeast corner room.

Jerry Solem, owner of the restaurant and saloon Norwood Pines, said:

The legend of the place says that a couple was making love in that first floor room. Apparently, there was jealousy involved on the part of a local gangster. [One] night he crashed the party, firing away, killing both [the] rival and the prostitute.

Some Capone-era gangsters liked to come to Norwood Pines. They could relax here. One of the Capones—maybe Al—said one of his favorite times was attending the wedding of a relative here.

Today, Norwood Pines is one of the finest restaurants in the Northwoods.

Green Bay Wants Its Booze

On October 19, 1928, the locals of Green Bay were outraged by the city council's decision to padlock 49 saloons in that northeastern Wisconsin city.

The local press noted that the padlocking of the 49 saloons was getting nationwide publicity. What was happening [after that] in Green Bay was called a "revolt" of sorts. The Chicago *Tribune* commented, "The people of Green Bay want the federal government to leave its saloons alone."

Chicago radio station KYW told its listeners, "The Green Bay Packers were coming to Chicago on Sunday with a strong aerial attack, and no doubt, with a few resolutions."

The Green Bay local press concluded one of its articles on the uprising of the locals with "... some fanatical drys think the entire city council ought to be put in jail for passing that resolution."

A "dry" blasting the city council was not as odd as it might sound. The basic outcry was not even for the booze; 49 closed saloons meant less people entering—and spending money—in the business district. The people were outraged at the collapse to their economy!

The city council rescinded the padlock resolution on October 24, 1928.

Still on Peake's Point Confiscated

It wasn't just the selling of alcohol that boosted the economy in the Northwoods; making the alcohol was also "big business."

On October 22, 1928 a still was discovered by federal prohibition agents working out of Milwaukee on the "Old Smith Farm" near Peake's Point on the west shore of Green Bay. The still was valued at $30,000 and the supply of mash it contained was sufficient to produce $93,000 worth of alcohol at the prices of the times.

On October 24, 1928, the headlines of the Green Bay *Press-Gazette* told that the still was being dismantled. As one of the supposedly empty steel tanks was being cut down with an acetylene torch, a stream of pure grain alcohol gushed forth. The fluid ignited and the blaze was extinguished with difficulty. The fire was finally brought under control by smothering it with wet sacks ... grain sacks, most likely.

New Lisbon's Big Still

On November 28, 1928, five stills—one of them the largest yet to be found in Wisconsin—were taken over by state and federal prohibition agents after a running gun battle with seven men who were bent on keeping the still. This was in an AP story datelined in Mauston, Wisconsin.

The largest of the stills at New Lisbon, Wisconsin, was valued at $75,000.00 and considered among the largest ever confiscated.

In addition to a speed wagon type of truck loaded with 1,400 gallons of alcohol, equipment found in the barn included two boilers used to run the stills, two stills—one of 1,000-gallon capacity and the other 100 gallons—and 11 vats of 5,000-gallon capacity each, located in the basement. All vats except one were filled with mash.

Agents also found "25 or 30 flashlights" scattered in sections of the barn. Perhaps the moonshiners were into a little moonlighting.

Opposite page:
Federal officer shown looking over a 25,000-gallon alcohol distilling plant found by members of Chicago's Alcohol Tax Unit September 19, 1935, on the tenth floor of Loop Office Building only two blocks from the ATU offices. The Feds were tipped off to the location of the still by the owners of the building. *AP/Wide World photos.*

The Phantom Still of Langlade County

The date was April 30, 1935. "The ghost of a huge Langlade County alcohol still . . . stalked here today," wrote the Green Bay *Press-Gazette* in its Tuesday evening edition.

> . . . And the ghost talked, its words unfolding a weird tale of a phantom-like still, one that has flourished almost unhampered through Prohibition since, without being raided, a still that has been shrouded in avarice and tainted with bribery, with hijacking and probably even murder as it smeared further the already filthy trail of the illicit liquor trade which sprang with Prohibition.
>
> Two Green Bay men are in state prison today because of that still. Herb Schroeder and Edwin Neuman . . . were in the hijacking racket and had to steal automobiles . . ."

The major still was located on the "Langlois Farm," a 320-acre, densely wooded tract about 12 miles north of Antigo, Wisconsin, and a couple of miles from the main highway.

One of the characters in the phantom still story was "Stub" Granger. He told Attorney Clement W. Dwyer of Green Bay that the Antigo still had once been located near Appleton, later near Shawano, and for several years now at the Langlade County site.

One of the major questions posed by the search for the still and, later, at the trial of Schroeder and Neuman was whether Walter Nier, who was murdered in his home on March 14th, was done in by the gang or by the federal agents. In the report on Nier, two men, posing as federal agents came to his home about 1:00 a.m. and opened fire on him when he refused to "go for a ride" with them. Nier's wife and two sons were narrowly missed by the flying .45 slugs.

It was well known that Nier was a hijacker—undoubtedly tied up with Schroeder and others. He had previously been shot in July, 1932, near Krakow, but recovered. He claimed then that he had been mistaken for a hijacker by bootleggers who were operating a still. Nier's assassins were never found.

The other interesting question that was a part of the phantom still involved the double murder of Paddy Berrell and Willie Marks, Chicago hoodlums and union men whose bodies were riddled by machine gun fire at the Lime Kiln Inn on Highway 29, about midway between Bonduel and Shawano. Berrell, 50, an official of the Chicago teamsters' and chauffeurs' union and Marks, said to be a survivor of the St. Valentine's Day Massacre had registered at the Lime Kiln Inn. Berrell, it was determined, was on holiday as a result of the "Red" Barker slaying in Chicago. His gangland enemies had followed Marks' car to the inn. In some way, officials connected these deaths with the phantom still and mob activity in the area.

Meanwhile, the search for the Langlade County alcohol still went on. But it seemed to be able to move without leaving a trace. It was massive, with large mash storage tanks, three boiler stacks and a long shed. It also contained a quantity of alcohol cans. By no means was it an easy thing to move. For such a large facility, it was surprising that no raid had ever been made on it.

Sobieski's Still

In March 1935 federal agents discovered a large still in operation in Sobieski, Wisconsin. The road to get to the still was through a swamp. It was so much of a mire that March day that the federal and state agents had to push their vehicles up to the still to make their raid.

The still operators, of course, had plenty of time to escape, fleeing into the swamp. The Feds, however, were able to confiscate the 500-gallon plant for converting high-test "moon" into alcohol. They also seized a steam boiler, a copper cooker, two copper columns and 150 gallons of the illicit product.

The Capture of a Rum Runner, Sturgeon Bay, Wisconsin

In 1928, a "rum running" ship known as the *Geronimo* was seized and forfeited. Although not a speedy ship, the *Geronimo* pulled a fast one after the seizure. It had been tied by Feds to a mooring at Fort Wayne, an Army post near Detroit, Michigan, and was in the custody of the United States marshal. But one night the hawsers were found cut, and the next morning, the *Geronimo* was riding anchor on the Canadian side of the river.

American authorities, in two tugs, started across the river to tow the *Geronimo* back. The rum runners protested, saying "They're chasing us with gunboats!" Well, the Canadian government told the United States to back off, especially since it was discovered that there was a Canadian admiralty lien on the boat.

On Thursday, May 15, 1930, the *Geronimo*, now renamed the *Amherstberg* (or *Ansterberg*), was again captured for rum running. The cargo of 4,000 cases of Canadian ale was valued at $20 per case for a market value of $80,000. (Another report listed the value of the cargo at $65 per case for a market value in the Green Bay area at $260,000.)

The rum running boat was escorted by the Plum Island U.S. Coast Guard to Sturgeon Bay. They were greeted by a tremendous crowd of spectators. What was interesting was that the crowd wasn't cheering the Coast Guard for their valiant effort in capturing the vessel in the illegal act of rum running; the crowd was cheering for the rum runners! One of the arrested rum runners commented, "We've got enough money back of us to buy Sturgeon Bay and Door County."

The funny thing was, especially at that point of the Depression, they probably did.

Rum Running in Preble, Wisconsin

It was May 27, 1930, when William J. "Bill" Miller, Preble, Wisconsin soft drink parlor owner, issued a "not guilty" plea when arraigned before U.S. Commissioner John F. Watermolen on a charge of conspiracy to violate the Prohibition law. He was being held under a $5,000 bond. Miller was charged with conspiracy with Walter F. Wilhelm, John Vanderbusch and other persons to smuggle 500 cases of Canadian beer and ale into the United States by way of the St. Mary's River. The plan, according to the indictment, was to load the contraband in the motorboat *Dryad* at Blind River, Ontario, and then run it down the St. Mary's River through Lakes Huron and Michigan to Manitowoc, Wisconsin.

The *Dryad*, with Wilhelm at the helm, was loaded at Blind River on August 22nd. The craft then headed for Sault Ste. Marie, Michigan, with its cargo consigned to a "C. Freeman," believed to be Miller's alias.

On August 23rd the boat was seized in the Straits of Mackinac, running without lights. The beer was discovered and arrests were made.

Hayward, Hurley and Hell!

Hurley—Still No Angel, a book by Lewis C. Reimann, gives some indication of the mining and lumberjack towns in the Northwoods of Wisconsin:

> Throughout the middle west, wherever lumberjacks and miners gathered, Hurley was known as the "hell-hole" of the Iron Range. Even Seney, Michigan, at its worst and liveliest, could not compete with the concentrated sin, suffering and saloons that gave Hurley a reputation unrivaled from Detroit to Duluth. "The four worst places in the world are Cumberland, Hayward, Hurley and Hell," it was said, "and Hurley was the toughest of all."
>
> The six-block heart of Silver Street had 65 liquor-dispensing places.

That was the cry in the '30s. Hayward today gets little notice that it too had a reputation that rivaled Hurley's. Hurley is located at the top of Wisconsin where Highway 51 ends. Nearby is The Hideout,

Peter De Rubies, a former mayor of Hurley with the book *Hurley— Still No Angel* that recalls the "good ol' days" when Hurley was alive and kicking. *Tom Hollatz photo.*

Al Capone's vacation retreat with its small "recreational" lake where rum running planes landed and, it is believed, some of Big Al's enemies found watery graves.

The Old World's End Resort was reported to have housed a gangster or two in the 1930s. One long-time resident said "Greasy Thumb" Guzik, the Capone mob financial manager, stayed there. The old resort was located on the northeast end of Chief Lake, on the 17,248-acre Chippewa Flowage, one of the better musky areas in the world.

Also on the "Big Chip" was another Chicago mobster, Johnny Moore. The story locals tell is that "he was in on the St. Valentine's Day Massacre . . . not many people know that either . . ." then there was "Radio Joe's" one of the first-class motels in the Northwoods. The owner, Joe Szumowski, reportedly married into the Joe Saltis family (which had a retreat north of Winter, Wisconsin, on Barker Lake).

On May 19, 1923, the most notorious saloon and gambling joint in the Northwoods was raided by the authorities. The Board of Trade Bar in Hurley was gutted by the Feds. Once known as the most elite of saloons, the Prohibition era saw its "high-class" liquor replaced by raw moonshine and gin bucks. The second floor of the saloon was devoted entirely to gambling, and it was not uncommon to see as much as $5,000 in silver piled up in a corner where the blackjack and dice games were in progress. That second floor was arranged in rooms so that no one could command a full view of the gambling places from any one location.

Typical Northwoods beauty that attracted many gangsters. Long, shady roads, lots of woods, and the many lakes made for fun if left alone and good escapes if pursued. *Tom Hollatz photo.*

In one part of the Board of Trade, a bar and lunch counter served patrons who gambled for hours and never left the tables. Gambling was at such a height at one time that the owner of the building rented poker tables at $8.00 an hour.

A buzzer system connected the place to the police department. While the average person could not account for it, as soon as there was any sign of a disturbance, police arrived. After the trouble was quelled, the officers left as quickly and quietly as they had arrived.

Typical of the times, while the Board of Trade was comfortable selling illegal liquor, it also showed a humanitarian heart:

> Never a poor woman arrived at the place with a hard luck story that her husband had gambled away his pay but that Lytle [the owner] produced the money for her and did it smilingly. Never once did he hear of a family in distress that he didn't come to its aid.

But all that ended in March of 1923 when federal agents arrived and closed the Board of Trade. It was the first to be padlocked in Hurley.

Silver Street of Hurley was considered one of the most vice-ridden streets in the United States for several decades.

In the 1920s, the Capone mob reportedly ran a crime school there which survived as long as the mob remained in power.

The fascination with Hurley focused on its brothels and the so-called B-girls. Teenage girls were reportedly imported from Canada and from throughout the Midwest. The girls were schooled in the art of "mooching and dipping." After graduation, they were sent out to mob strongholds all over the United States.

The girls were lured to Hurley with the promise of dancing jobs. But when these teenagers arrived on Silver Street, the jobs were said to have gone. Penniless, they were told that it was easy picking up change by drinking with the honky-tonk customers. And if a customer just happened to get a little too drunk, he sure wouldn't miss a few bucks from his pocket. The girls who couldn't handle this routine were forced into prostitution.

Runaways were considered the most promising recruits and kept in virtual white slavery until they could no longer turn a profit. Girls who tried to flee were sometimes made an example of for the others to take notice. Beatings, knifings—even acid in the face—were part of the stiff curriculum of Hurley's crime school.

Tables Turned on Ironwood Sheriff

On November 13, 1929, the good folks of Ironwood, Michigan, were talking about their sheriff. The folks in Hurley (just across the border) were grinning.

The Associated Press had the story:

> Audience for years in a play of dry crusades, this city [Ironwood] found itself the chief actor.
>
> Accustomed to watch while state and federal governments attempted vainly to clean up the irrepressible lumber-mining town of Hurley, just across the border in Wisconsin, Ironwood was in a reverse role today. The sheriff John W. Johnson, was under arrest on a charge of conspiracy to violate the prohibition laws.
>
> While Hurley watched with amusement, despite the depressing influence of a new state clean-up, the sheriff was taken off to Marquette by federal agents and held in jail to await arraignment.

It seems that the sheriff sold beer to a Mrs. Mary Johnson of Marenisco, Michigan. She swore out an affidavit saying that she had bought beer from him. She probably didn't say that she had a nickname—Gyp the Blood—when she lived in Hurley.

Elcho, Wisconsin: First Aid Station

The quaint Northwood's community of Elcho on Highway 45 was known as the medical station for the hoods escaping to—and many times from—Wisconsin. It is said a mob doctor was always "taken care of" extremely well, with booze and cash, if he repaired wounded flesh. In the 1930s, a mob moll could also get a no-questions-asked abortion.

JOHN DILLINGER

How did a nation become enamored of a man like John Dillinger who was a bank robber at the very least, a vicious killer in truth (if even half of the murders attributed to him were his work)? The Dillinger era occurred at a time in history when the nation was trying to deal with the impossibility of Prohibition and the insanity of the stock market crash and the Great Depression.

On October 24, 1929—Black Thursday on Wall Street—stocks nose-dived amid a flurry of trading, some 13 million shares. In an attempt to head off the inevitable panic, the directors of several large banks met and later announced to the public that their confidence in the stock market was so strong that they were prepared to buy up stocks above their quoted price. In other words, the bankers were conning the papas and mammas of the United States who had invested their precious savings in the stock market. That public relations ploy held prices steady for five days. Then the bottom fell out.

Many blue chip securities fell 50 percent as tickers clacked for two awful hours after the closing bell just to keep up with the record volume traded—16 million shares! The losses, at least on paper, totaled $26,000,000,000.00. All the tiny little investments of all those everyday people, which was meant to be their comfortable retirements, was also gone. It was a devastating blow to the nation's economy and to the economy of every American who had dared to dream. They had believed what their helpful bankers had told them and

Photo courtesy the FBI.

23

had handed over their hard-earned cash. Now it was all gone, and people were angry.

Along comes John Dillinger. A crook. But a very significant kind of crook—a bank robber. In the eyes of many Americans, getting back at the banks was part of their revenge fantasies. John Dillinger acted them out. It's no wonder the nation accepted, even embraced, the Dillinger gang, Ma Barker and her boys, Bonnie and Clyde and the others who preyed on banks. It could almost be forgotten that people died in the process of robbing banks, that federal agents (they were part of the government that had let them down, right?) also died trying to apprehend the robbers, and sometimes innocent people were hurt or killed (innocent people died in war, too).

Dillinger's Troubled Youth

John Herbert Dillinger was born on June 22, 1903, to a hard-working grocer in Indianapolis, Indiana. John's mother died when he was three years old.

As a boy, Dillinger was an avid reader of Wild West stories. His favorite hero was Jesse James. According to his boyhood friend, Delbert Hobson, Dillinger thought Jesse James had Robin Hood qualities. He seemed obsessed not only with Jesse's courage and daring, but also with his kindness to women and children.

Dillinger was a good athlete, especially in baseball. He played shortstop and second base with ease. In John Toland's book, *The Dillinger Days*, Dillinger's hitting ability was described as savage— in practice. He rarely did well in actual games. Indiana Governor Harry Leslie watched one game when Dillinger played, fielding perfectly and hitting like a professional. The governor reportedly said, "That kid ought to be playing major league baseball." This athletic ability would be used later when robbing banks. It is said he could vault over counters easily.

When his father remarried, John was very resentful of his new stepmother. He began to act out. The family moved from the city to Mooresville, Indiana, in hopes that a smaller, more rural community setting would mitigate some of John's already troublesome behavior. But the break with the city did nothing to ease the tension between John and his father. The theft of an auto led John to enlist in the Navy. But, as Fireman 3rd class, John Dillinger ended his naval career by jumping ship, the *U.S.S. Utah*, and deserting.

Back in Mooresville, he married sixteen-year-old Beryl Hovius in 1924. The newlyweds headed to Indianapolis but John could not find work. He was soon befriended by Ed Singleton, whom the FBI later labeled "the town pool shark."

Dillinger and Singleton attempted to rob a Mooresville grocer.

"Never trust an automatic pistol or a D.A.'s deal."
—JOHN DILLINGER

John Dillinger. *FBI photo.*

The man was badly beaten. Singleton got a two year sentence. Dillinger received joint sentences (for the robbery and the assault) of 2 to 14 years and 10 to 20 years in the Indiana State Prison. Stunned by the harsh sentences, Dillinger became a bitter man in prison.

Ten Months of Terror

Nine years later, he emerged from prison on parole "determined to get even with society." Within four months of his release, he had robbed eight banks and added some $100,000 to his fortune. Dillinger was feeling a little cocky with his success and helped some of his former cronies escape from prison on September 26, 1933. Dillinger was soon captured by Ohio police and placed in the County Jail at Lima, Ohio. But the escaped convicts—Harry Pierpont, Russell Clark and Charles Makley—returned the favor. On the night of October 12, 1933, they beat and killed Sheriff Jess Sarber. Dillinger escaped.

From September 1933 until July 1934, Dillinger and his gang stormed through the Midwest, killing 10 men, wounding seven others, robbing banks and police arsenals, and staging three jail breaks. The police arsenals yielded several machine guns, rifles and revolvers, ammunition, and bulletproof vests.

On December 14, 1933, John Hamilton, a Dillinger gang member, shot and killed a police officer during the robbery of the First National Bank of East Chicago, Indiana. Then they made their way to Florida, then to Tucson, Arizona. In Tucson, on January 23, 1934, a fire broke out in the hotel where gang members Russell Clark and Charles Makley were hiding under assumed names.

Firemen recognized them. Police nailed them, taking Dillinger and Harry Pierpont in the same sweep. Officials seized three Thompson submachine guns, two Winchester rifles mounted as machine guns, five bulletproof vests, and more than $25,000 in cash.

Dillinger was returned to the county jail at Crown Point, Indiana, awaiting trial for the murder of the East Chicago police officer. But on March 3, 1934, Dillinger cowed the jail guards with what he admitted later was a wooden gun that he had whittled. He grabbed two machine guns and locked up the guards. He was loose again.

Another shot of Dillinger. *FBI photo.*

The FBI Get in on the Action

Oddly enough, although Dillinger had robbed banks, killed at least one man, staged jail breaks, and escaped himself, he had not violated any federal law. But by escaping in the sheriff's car and crossing from Indiana into Illinois on his way to Chicago, he violated the National Motor Vehicle Theft Act, which stated that it was a federal offense to transport a stolen motor vehicle across state lines. A grand jury returned an indictment against Dillinger. The FBI received the green light to become actively involved in the nationwide search for Dillinger.

In Chicago, Dillinger joined up with his girl friend, Evelyn "Billie" Frechette. Together they headed for the "safe" city of St. Paul, Minnesota, where he teamed up with Homer Van Meter, Lester "Baby Face Nelson" Gillis, Eddie Green, and Tommy Carroll, among others. This was the evening of March 4, 1934.

Within two days of Dillinger's arrival in St. Paul, Green suggested they rob a bank in Sioux Falls, South Dakota. On Tuesday, March 6, 1934, Dillinger's gang drove to South Dakota and robbed the Security National Bank and Trust Company of $49,000 cash. They returned to St. Paul to split the money and lay low for the next few days.

On March 13th Dillinger and his gang robbed the First National Bank of Mason City, Iowa. The bank's security was stronger than anticipated. Eddie Green, well-known as the "jug maker," was hit by a shot from a tear gas gun. A police magistrate on the third floor

John Dillinger and members of his gang during arraignment in Tuscon, Arizona. This was the last time that "Public Enemy No. 1" was taken alive. *National Archives' photo.*

of an office building shot Dillinger in the shoulder as he was leading some bank customers out into the street. John Hamilton was also wounded. According to an FBI reporter Ed Riege of the Minneapolis office, Dillinger and his gang fled Mason City by forcing some of the bank customers to stand on the running boards of their getaway car.

The gang returned to St. Paul where Dillinger and Hamilton received medical attention from a St. Paul doctor. Then Dillinger and Billie Frechette moved into an apartment (303) of the Lincoln Court apartments at 93 South Lexington Avenue. They used the names of Mr. and Mrs. Carl T. Hellman.

Thanks to a suspicious apartment manager, two federal agents, R. C. Coulter and R. L. Nails, began an investigation on March 30th.

On March 31st, Agent Coulter, along with St. Paul detective Henry Cummings, approached the apartment while Agent Nails remained outside on the street.

Billie opened the door, saw the men and yelled "Feds!" She slammed the door in their faces. In the madness that followed, Dillinger, Frechette and Van Meter escaped, meeting in the rear of the apartment complex and escaping in a 1934 Hudson. Dillinger had been hit in the leg.

The threesome fled to Minneapolis, seeking shelter with Eddie Green. There Dillinger received medical attention from Minneapolis doctor, Clayton May.

After the March 31st shootout, an intensive FBI manhunt was launched in the Minneapolis-St. Paul area. A break occurred for them on April 3rd when agents confronted the cleaning lady outside apartment 303. She confessed to them that she was under instructions to retrieve Dillinger's suitcase. The FBI let her do just that.

Dillinger, thinking. *FBI photo.*

With agents staked out around the cleaning woman's home, the FBI hoped to trap Dillinger. But it was Eddie Green who entered the house, grabbed the suitcase and raced for his car. He was ordered to stop. Green spun around and reached for one of his two revolvers in shoulder holsters. An agent stationed at the dining room window of the house fired, sending Green sprawling. He died on April 11th.

On April 8th, John Dillinger and his beloved Billie travelled back to Chicago. There Frechette was arrested. She confessed to being with Dillinger on March 31st in the St. Paul apartment. In May, 1934, a St. Paul Federal jury convicted Frechette of conspiracy to harbor a fugitive. She was sentenced to serve two years in the Woman's Federal Prison at Milan, Michigan.

After Billie's arrest, Dillinger left Chicago to meet with Homer Van Meter. At approximately 1:30 a.m., the two men forced a night police officer to open the police station in Warsaw, Indiana. They stole machine guns and bulletproof vests.

Dillinger regrouped with Baby Face, Tommy Carroll, John Hamilton, and Van Meter. On Friday, April 20th, a sixth individual, Pat Riley, a St. Paul gangland errand boy, joined them. He led the gang to a small resort in the Spider Lake (Manitowish Waters), Wisconsin, area. Here, in the restful and lovely Northwoods of Wisconsin, the gang could lie low for a while until the Feds backed off. The place where they stayed was called Little Bohemia.

A faded photograph of the sign of Little Bohemia as it appeared when John Dillinger visited there. *Tom Hollatz photo.*

Little Bohemia

Dillinger was making the Feds look like fools. Not only was he pulling off many jobs, but was escaping right from under the noses of everyone . . . time and time again. It had been expected that once the FBI got into the action, that Dillinger would have just about held up his hands and begged for mercy. That didn't exactly happen. Instead, Dillinger's crime spree seemed to be escalating. While he was seen as clever, cunning and daring, the Feds were beginning to look like bumbling idiots. This was not an image J. Edgar Hoover wanted for the fledgling FBI. So, when they got a tip from a resort owner that Dillinger was at Little Bohemia, they had a lot riding on a successful capture or elimination of "Public Enemy No. 1."

But what happened one night at Little Bohemia in Manitowish Waters would become part of American lore, forever carving Dillinger's name in a gangster litany of sorts that belongs to the ages.

The entire "get Dillinger" scenario began to take form on Sunday, April 22, 1934, when two planes from Chicago touched down at Rhinelander airport. Aboard were Melvin Purvis and other FBI agents. The plane from the St. Paul bureau was already on the ground. It carried Assistant Director H. Hugh Clegg, who was now counting his troops, some 17 in all. Local wardens and constables

The entrance to Little Bohemia on Highway 51 in Manitowish Waters, Wisconsin. Here startled federal agents opened up on three customers who were leaving after the Sunday night chicken dinner. Thinking the car contained Dillinger and some gang members, Melvin Purvis directed his agents to fire. Three locals were wounded, one of which—Eugene Boiseneau—was killed. *Tom Hollatz photo.*

would be added later when the Dillinger dragnet was triggered.

Clegg was first in command, and Purvis, second. One agent returned with Henry Voss to his resort, which would be the staging area for the attack. Later, the remaining agents followed in rented cars, turning north at Woodruff on Highway 51.

The plan was for Emil Wanatka Sr., the owner of Little Bohemia resort, to herd whoever was inside the building into the basement at about 4:00 a.m. It was hoped other Feds would have had time to drive from St. Paul to block roads before the assault. But word had gotten out that Dillinger planned to leave after dinner on Sunday night and not on the 23rd as the Feds hoped. They rushed to adjust their plans.

It was a cold trip out of Rhinelander in the five cars. When two of the clunkers broke down, several agents climbed on running boards. Armed with an assortment of weapons, it was no easy task, especially on that frigid night. The road was muddy; deep holes made it a difficult trip.

At Birchwood Lodge, Voss's resort on Highway 51 near Little Bohemia, Clegg organized his men for a quick assault, fearing Dillinger was going to flee, and soon.

The agents set out in three cars with all lights out—and all cig-

Little Bohemia. Owned at the time of the escape by Emil Wanatka, Sr., later by his son Emil, and now the resort is owned by Fred and Terry Theisen. *Tom Hollatz photo.*

arettes were doused. They headed northwest on Highway 51.

At the entrance to Little Bohemia, a good distance from the main lodge on Little Star Lake, Clegg ordered two of the cars to block the entrance in a V formation.

The agents spread out on both sides of the entrance, each wearing a 24-pound bulletproof vest. It's a wonder none were sucked under in the mud on that cold April night.

It should be pointed out that the Feds were totally unfamiliar with Little Bohemia. Voss scribbled a map that left out three main factors.

1. There was a ditch to the left of the lodge.
2. There was a fence on the right.
3. There was a steep bank near the lake. (I never realized that there was a steep bank on the shore even as a frequent diner at Little Bohemia. It was only when I attended a sailing regatta on the shore that I got a sense of the steepness, a perfect shield and cover for

anyone who walked—or ran—along the shoreline.)

Inside, Dillinger was playing cards with his men in the bar.

Outside, the Wanatkas' two collies started barking.

Something in the darkness sparked their yelping. Dillinger didn't even look up.

Three local diners, a gas salesman from Mercer and two men from the local CCC camp, decided to leave.

Inside the noisy car augmented by a crackling loud radio, the three men felt good after the $1.00 Sunday night chicken dinner, a favorite offering of the Wanatkas.

The dogs continued barking. Bartenders Frank Traube and George Bazso stepped outside to see what, if anything, was causing the dogs to bark.

The agents watched as the three men entered the car and Traube and Bazso stood at one side. Seeing five men emerge, the agents thought it was an alerted Dillinger and his gang ready to flee. They got ready.

The car carrying John Hoffman, the gas station attendant, John Morris, a CCC cook, and Eugene Boiseneau, a CCC specialist, drove slowly along the long pine tree-lined entrance to Highway 51. The car's lights bounced through the blackness as the wheels found the frequent potholes.

Fearing the gang was trying to escape, Clegg and Purvis ordered their men to open fire—first at the tires. The three occupants of the car did not hear the command to "halt," and the car continued to move.

It was then all hell broke loose as the agents, using .38s and Thompson submachine guns, fired at will.

John Morris, hit four times by FBI bullets, spilled from the passenger's side of the car. Shaking in terror, he fled back to the lodge. Morris grabbed the bar phone and called Alvin Koerner. "Alvin, I'm at Emil's. Everybody here has been knocked out." With that, Morris collapsed.

Hoffman, also wounded, stumbled from the driver's side and crawled to the safety of the nearby woods. Slumped in the middle seat was Gene Boiseneau, 35. He was staring straight ahead at the blood-drenched dashboard, killed instantly in the first volley.

Inside, Dillinger and his men scrambled away with precision.

Dillinger, Homer Van Meter, Tommy Carroll, and John Hamilton headed for an upstairs window and escaped via the roof facing the lake. They ran to the right.

Baby Face Nelson, in a nearby cabin with his wife, stayed a few moments, reportedly firing two pistols at a figure with a submachine gun believed to be Melvin Purvis. He missed. Purvis' weapon jammed. Nelson ran for the lake, exchanging fire with Purvis, now using a .38. Nelson escaped along the shoreline.

Prince and Spot, the collies that probably alerted Dillinger and his gang to the fact that the Feds were closing in. Shown here with their owner, Mrs. Nan Wanatka. *AP/Wide World photo.*

Special Agent Melvin Purvis (left) and his boss, FBI director J. Edgar Hoover. Purvis was in charge of the Little Bohemia operation, but instead of capturing Dillinger, Purvis' men opened fire on three local men. *FBI photo.*

Wanatka and the three molls ran for the basement. The girls would remain there until the following morning. Clegg ordered a ceasefire. In the madness of the assault, some agents who were flanking Little Bohemia fell into the ditch to the left. Those on the right ran into the barbed-wire fence. It was chaos.

Clegg ordered a ceasefire.

It was quiet, ominously so.

It would be several hours before the Feds would teargas the lodge and then break in. A somewhat befuddled Purvis, who would later commit suicide, for some reason would not believe Emil Wanatka Sr., who had been at Alvin Koerner's when Nelson unleashed his terror on agents W. Carter Baum and Jay Newman. Constable Carl Christensen was also struck in that momentary fury.

It was over.

Dillinger and his men were gone.

The public outcry was just beginning.

What would follow would be the most intense manhunt by the Feds in United States history.

Inside Little Bohemia Emil Wanatka's Story

Emil Wanatka Sr., the owner of Little Bohemia, saw the events of that Sunday night from a different angle than the federal agents at the gate.

Last Friday afternoon [April 20, 1934] one man and a woman came here and asked for accommodations. I showed them the rooms, and they said more people were coming. About two hours later another car came in. There were three men and a woman in that machine, and later another auto came with two men and two women. Later, one woman and a man left in one of the cars.

Dillinger came in the second car. All were well dressed and very polite. "My name is John Dillinger. We are going to stay here a few days," Dillinger told Wanatka.

Protests were quieted with a surly order "not to talk back."

Frank Traube [one of Wanatka's employees] said he recognized Dillinger "the minute he stepped into the room."

Once Dillinger and his crowd were settled, we couldn't complain about them even though we were virtually held prisoners. They were pleasant enough to all of us. They acted like any other guests do at a summer hotel. The only difference was that the men always carried guns. When they played poker, they put their weapons on the table. Dillinger invited me to play with them. They weren't cheapskates. It was a real game. Those boys had money.

On Saturday [the 21st] they got up about 8:30 and had breakfast, and just loafed around, taking walks about the grounds and reading. Today I found two books: *The Little Shepherd of Kingdom Come* and

George Bazso, 81, who with his wife Mabel operates Hillcrest Resort on the Manitowish chain of lakes, was the bartender of the Little Bohemia the night John Dillinger and his gang fled from the FBI.

Bazso and Frank Traube were on duty together that night. "It was my turn to wait on tables," Bazso said. "I brought a piece of apple pie to Baby Face Nelson. I called him 'Jimmy' because he liked it. He wanted another piece and I got it for him. He gave me a $5.00 tip. I brought him one more piece, and he gave me another $5.00."

Later, Bazso and Traube went outside to see why Emil's two black collies were barking. At the same time, the three men from Mercer were leaving.

Little did they know that waiting outside were dozens of FBI men and local law enforcement personnel.

When the shooting started, Bazso said, "I ran like hell to the basement. The shooting lasted only 15 minutes and that was it. Nothing like all night as portrayed in several movies."

After the shooting, he, Emil Sr. and George LaPorte, drove to the nearby home of Alvin Koerner on Highway 51. He operated the local telephone exchange. Once inside the Koerner home, they spotted Baby Face holding a .45 on the Koerners and some friends.

Bazso said, "Hello, Jimmy."

"Never mind the bullshit," Nelson shot back. "Just line up against the wall."

Nelson forced Wanatka, Koerner and Bazso outside and into what was to be the get-away car. Just then, a car pulled in off the highway.

"Baby Face walked right to their car. He saw their machine guns across their laps and immediately opened fire."

In the exchange, one man was killed and the others wounded.

"Nelson got in their car and headed south on 51. It was a souped up model that could hit 103 mph. He was gone."

Bazso's reputation as a guide has brought him more fame than that brief encounter with Dillinger, Nelson and the gang. And he likes it that way.

As he showed some old photos that included a 36-pound musky and a mammoth 45-pound one, he turned and said, "Come to think of it, I could have been killed that night." *Tom Hollatz photo.*

Murder on the Yacht. [They were] in the room Dillinger occupied. They liked to read magazines and newspapers. Saturday night we played poker again, and I won about $28.

The men drank beer and fizzies, but the girls didn't drink much. But they smoked a lot.

I didn't sleep well while they were here. My wife got nervous, and yesterday she went over to her sister's house and stayed there.

All of them [the gangsters] liked to eat, they praised Mrs. Wanatka's cooking. The girls made up the beds, saying they knew we were short of help this time of year. The girls were good looking, and I thought they were about 20 or 22 years old. They all seemed happy while here.

I read that Dillinger limped because of a wound he received when he escaped in St. Paul, but I didn't notice it while he was here.

Dillinger's pals called him John. Others I remember were called Bill, Red, Jim and Curley.

All day Sunday they just loafed around again, and two of the men took one of the automobiles and were gone for about two hours.

When the shooting started last night [Sunday night, April 22], I [had just finished] with three customers: Morris, Boiseneau—the boy who was killed—and Hoffman. [At the sound of shots being fired], I ran downstairs to the basement with the three girls and my two waiters. The girls were nervous and screamed and cried. They seemed brokenhearted.

After a while when the shooting quieted down, I went up the outside cellar steps with my two waiters. We had our hands up above our heads, and the federal men sent us over to Koerner's.

The girls were willing to surrender, but no one seemed to pay attention to them when they cried, "Don't shoot, we'll come out."

A bullet-shattered window at the Little Bohemia after the bungled attempt to capture Dillinger on the snowy Sunday night of April 22, 1934. *Camera/100 Collection.*

Rare photo of an unknown man pointing out the bullet holes blasted by the FBI into the car with the three local men. Thinking the car contained Dillinger and his men, the Feds opened fire with submachine gun fire, killing one of the men and wounding two others. *Camera/100 Collection photo.*

They stayed down in the basement until about 6:00 this morning when the tear gas bombs were tossed into the building.

It was a terrible night.

The federal officers confiscated six machine guns, a dozen shotguns and rifles and five steel vests. They also took 15 bags belonging to the gang.

The Morning After

John Dillinger and Baby Face Nelson's great escape on Sunday, April 22, was big news the morning after.

Sheriff's forces throughout upper Wisconsin and 12 deputies from St. Louis County were ordered out to guard all roads. Sheriff Frank Carlson was organizing a force of 20 deputies to join the hunt. Requests for Wisconsin national guard troops were sent to Rhinelander.

After shooting their way out of a beer tavern late last night, Dillinger and his companions . . . fled in two automobiles, one a Packard and the other a Ford sedan.

. . . It was reported that 27 department of justice men participated in the elaborate trap and subsequent gun-fight.

It could not be established how many persons were in the resort when the battle started.

. . . Werner Hanni, chief of the department of justice for the northwest, H. H. Clegg and A. W. Roper, inspectors and other federal agents early today left St. Paul for northern Wisconsin to aid in the hunt for John Dillinger.

The Associated Press, in a story datelined Sault Ste. Marie, Michigan, April 22: John Dillinger and his first lieutenant, John Hamilton, apparently were reunited tonight after several months supposed separation in the hiding from law-enforcement agents.

The same day that the Feds botched the "Dillinger job," at Little Bohemia, his girlfriend, Evelyn Frechette, was arriving in St. Paul by plane. The Associated Press:

While heavily-armed federal and police details, alert against the possibility of a rescue attempt, kept visitors away, Evelyn Frechette, half-Indian sweetheart of John Dillinger, arrived here today by airplane from Chicago.

Facing charges of harboring the Indiana badman and aiding his escape from a St. Paul apartment several weeks ago, the woman was whirled away in an automobile and lodged in the county jail.

Leaving behind a blood-stained trail across the blizzard-swept wilds of northern Wisconsin . . . from the Little Bohemia resort near Mercer where two men were killed and four wounded Sunday, tracks of the desperadoes were traced to the outskirts of St. Paul last night where the car in which Dillinger himself escaped was

found blood-stained.

"The car bore stains which indicated at least one member of the gang, possibly Dillinger himself, had been seriously wounded earlier in the day in a running battle with deputy officers near Hastings, Minnesota.

"Striking with the ferocity of a wounded tiger seeking its lair, three of the Dillinger mobsters blasted their way through a cordon protecting the southeast approach to St. Paul, according to the Associated Press . . ."

George "Baby Face" Nelson fled left (south) from Little Bohemia along the shore of Little Star Lake of the Manitowish Waters' chain. Dillinger and the rest scrambled down the steep embankment to the right (north) after the botched capture attempt. *Tom Hollatz photo.*

Trail of the Escape

Meanwhile, three other persons who talked with Dillinger during his escape were recounting their unwilling parts in the affair. These people were: Robert Johnson, 25, who was kidnapped by the ring leader and two others of the gang and forced to drive them on

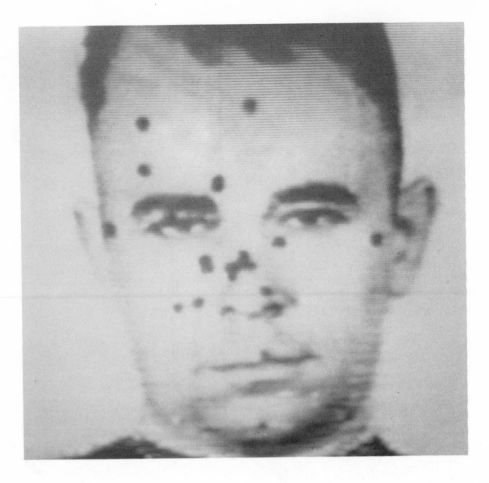

Rare photo of one of the targets resembling John Dillinger that federal agents practiced on after the famous gangster fled Little Bohemia on April 22, 1934. *FBI photo.*

a getaway trip . . . and Mr. and Mrs. E. J. Mitchell, proprietors of Mitchell's Resort, also near Little Bohemia, where Mr. Johnson had a cabin.

Mitchell, a sturdy farmer type, said he and his wife talked with Dillinger for about 20 minutes.

> I heard a knock on the door before 10:00 last night [Sunday, April 22], and when I opened it I saw John Dillinger and two other men. Dillinger told me his name. One of the other men was carrying a machine gun hugged close to his body.
>
> Dillinger said, "I'm John Dillinger, the federal men are after me, and I want a car."
>
> I pointed to an old truck in the shed, and he said, "Maybe that will work."
>
> Just then my wife came to the door, and he told us to get outside. I told him my wife had been sick, and she should have something around her. He said, "Oh, that's all right," and stepped on the porch and got a blanket which he put around my wife's shoulders. "Come on, mother," he said, "you'll be all right."
>
> My man, Eric Tobehn, tried to get the truck started, but couldn't. Then Dillinger saw a coupe next to it and asked who it belonged to. I told him Robert Johnson. He asked where Robert Johnson lived, and

FBI director J. Edgar Hoover prepares to test fire a deadly Thompson submachine gun. The 1911A1 Thompson can unleash 600 .45-caliber rounds per minute. Catching the gangsters of the 1930s, especially Public Enemy No. 1 John Dillinger, became an obsession with him. *FBI photo.*

I pointed out his cottage, so then Dillinger went over and got Johnson out of bed. Johnson started his car, and the men got in, and they drove off.

Mitchell and his wife added that Dillinger behaved "like a gentleman."

Johnson revealed how he was forced to drive the three men to a point 12 miles south of Park Falls, Wisconsin, where they put him out of the car with a warning to "Keep walking until morning."

Two of the men got in the seat with me, and the other climbed into the rumble seat. During the entire drive they didn't talk much, but told me once in a while to keep the accelerator pressed to the floor. I didn't waste any time either. We stopped once at a filling station to get gas and ask directions. They avoided traveled roads.

I didn't think much about being scared, but they kept a gun pointed at me all the time. I was wearing only bedroom slippers, and when they put me out of the car, I walked four miles to a power station where I telephoned for help.

Johnson had driven some 50 miles before Dillinger and his men dropped him off.

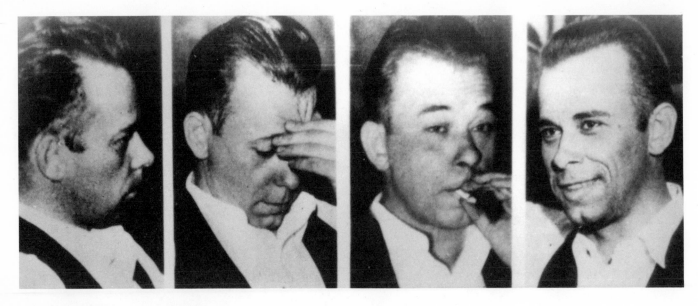

The many faces of the most wanted criminal in the world in the 1930s, John Herbert Dillinger. *FBI photo.*

April 27, 1934

The Daily Press newspaper, Ashland, Wisconsin.
Headline: **Dillinger Gunmen Near Fifield**

State highways 70 and 13 put under guard.

Sheriff Hennell and Undersheriff Freeman of Ashland County began patrolling the highways leading into Ashland when reports were received that Baby Face Nelson of the Dillinger Gang was headed for Ashland in a stolen car. Ashland Police Chief Saunders was also aiding in the search.

"Well, they had Dillinger surrounded and was all ready to shoot him when he come, but another bunch of folks come out ahead, so they just shot them instead. Dillinger is going to accidentally get with some bystanders some time, then he will get shot . . ."
WILL ROGERS

April 28, 1934

The Daily Press, Ashland, Wisconsin.
Headline: **Baby Face Is Hunted Here**

Al Johnson, special deputy, reported at Superior he believed he had wounded Nelson in an exchange of shots near Solon Springs. The deputy was wounded slightly.

Public Enemy No. 1

When Dillinger escaped from Little Bohemia, the FBI suffered a serious disgrace. And when, in the next few weeks, they were still unable to capture the criminal—although there were numerous sightings—their credibility fell. J. Edgar Hoover was obsessed with the capture of Dillinger and bent on regaining the prestige position of the FBI. Dillinger was Public Enemy No. 1. He was the most sought after criminal in the United States.

But nothing seemed to be working. Dillinger had vanished from the Wisconsin Northwoods, slipped past dozens of FBI agents and all the available law enforcement personnel in the area. It was not until some time later that the FBI had a break in the case.

The "Lady in Red"

When Dillinger went to see "Manhattan Melodrama" at the Biograph Theater on July 22, 1934, Anna Sage was the famous "Lady in Red" who tipped off the FBI to the location of Public Enemy No. 1. (The dress was really orange, but it looked red under the neon lights of the Biograph.) Anna was the Judas at Dillinger's last supper.

Ms. Sage was a former madam and ran "houses" in Gary and East Chicago. She was a native of Romania and was threatened with deportation (perhaps because of her activities). Fearing this, Sage approached Sgt. Martin Zarkovich of the East Chicago police department; she wanted the deportation hearings dropped in exchange for delivering Dillinger into their hands.

Sgt. Zarkovich notified his superior, Capt. Timothy O'Malley, chief of detectives, who then contacted Melvin Purvis of the FBI. Purvis was special agent in charge of the FBI's Chicago office. He was eager to complete the capture of Dillinger that was such a dismal failure at Little Bohemia.

The Feds negotiated with Sage. While they couldn't promise to stop the deportation, they did say they would do what they could to prevent it. Her part of the bargain entailed becoming an operative for the FBI, and was paid through the Hargrave Agency. Hoover, who hated the fact that she was a "loose woman" so to speak, did not want a direct link with her even if he did want Dillinger. Sage was always paid in cash, and she did supply the FBI with good information on Dillinger . . . for a time. When the information began to drop off, however, there was a suspicion that she had fallen in love with the criminal.

But then, at 5:30 p.m. on Sunday, July 22, 1934, Sage called authorities. In hushed tones she said that she, Polly Hamilton, and John Dillinger were going out to a movie at either the Biograph or the Marbro theaters, she didn't know which one. Later, at 7:00 p.m., she called again and whispered that Dillinger was in the room with her, but she still didn't know which theatre.

The End at the Biograph Theater

The police and the FBI were already mobilized. Sgt. Zarkovich and his men staked out the Marbro Theater on Madison Street near Crawford Avenue (Pulaski Road now). Meanwhile, Purvis and his agents watched and waited at the Biograph Theater at 2433 North

The Biograph Theater, famous as the site where Dillinger was gunned down by the FBI, was urged by the Chicago landmark commission to submit an application that plays down the gangster connection and deals with the building's architectural history instead.

"We didn't want it to seem we were glorifying gangsterism," said project coordinator for the Commission on Chicago Historical and Architectural Landmarks.

Opened in 1915, the Biograph was the first movie theater built in Chicago, according to Larry Edwards, owner.

On July 22, 1934, after watching "Manhattan Melodrama," starring Clark Gable and William Powell, John Dillinger was gunned down by the FBI in an alley outside the theater.

Every year since Edwards has owned the theater, the Biograph has shown "Manhattan Melodrama" on July 22 and charged 25 cents, the 1934 price. *FBI photo.*

Lincoln Avenue.

At 10:30 p.m., when the "Manhattan Melodrama" ended, Purvis and his "West Side Team" were outside and ready. At this point, knowing that Dillinger would be willing to "resist" any attempts to arrest him, the men were ready to shoot to kill. This time, unlike the Little Bohemia encounter, the trap was set with precision and sprang shut almost anti-climactically. In just moments it was all over. Dillinger lay dead on the sidewalk, shot by agents Cowley and Hollis. Hoover had his pound of flesh.

It was over. The reign of terror across the nation that Dillinger waged was ended that hot July evening. Sage had done her job; she had given the FBI the chance it needed to dispose of Public Enemy No. 1. Her reward--she was deported and died in 1947. Purvis, who, it is said, loathed Hoover for welching on the deal with Sage, was so tormented by the outcome for the woman, took his own life in 1960.

As for Hollis and Cowley, who had dropped Dillinger, they later fatally wounded another of Dillinger's gang, Baby Face Nelson. On November 27, 1934, in a savage gun duel on Northwest Highway in Barrington, Illinois, Hollis and Cowley confronted Baby Face. It was said to be one of the fiercest gun battles ever waged between lawmen and gangsters. Baby Face died of his wounds later that night.

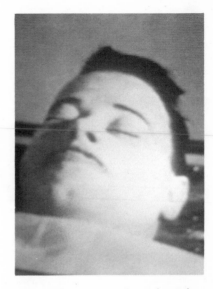

John Dillinger Dead! Girl Tricks Dillinger! These were some of the headlines after Dillinger was slain by federal agents near the Biograph Theater, July 22, 1934. *Camera/100 Collection.*

Missing Document

John Dillinger's autopsy report was considered one of the most important records of its kind in Chicago—the post-mortem of Public Enemy No. 1. But for a long time it was missing.

Nobody knows when the document, known as "A Coroner's Protocal," disappeared, but it is believed to have been missing since the late 1930s. After an absence of decades—almost 50 years to the date that Dillinger escaped from Little Bohemia—a clerk accidentally discovered it in a plain brown shopping bag in a room adjoining the office of Dr. Robert Stein, Cook County medical examiner, at 2121 West Harrison Street. The autopsy report was found by Christopher Morris, an administrative assistant to Stein, while rummaging through miscellaneous records in the Cook County Institute of Forensic Medicine.

How had it disappeared for so long? Was there a reason for this disappearance? The information in the autopsy itself also leads to questions.

The late Dr. Jerry Kerns, chief pathologist for Coroner Frank Walsh, performed the autopsy on John Dillinger the day after he was shot by the FBI. Dr. Kerns worked in the steaming, formaldehyde-reeking basement of the old county morgue at the corner of Polk and Wood streets.

The Dillinger Autopsy Report

History and cause of death: Gunshot. Removed from the sidewalk at 2450 Lincoln Avenue by 37th District police. Coroner's Docket Sheet Case No. 160747.

This information certainly jives with events outside the Biograph Theater.

The examination showed the presence of "rheumatic heart disease as a young man." Scalp and mustache hair had been "dyed black." Stein, the current medical examiner, explains this as part of Dillinger's disguise to elude police.

The report goes on to list that the dead man was 32 years old, five feet seven inches tall and weighed 160 pounds. But the first point was wrong. Dillinger had just turned 31; he was born June 22, 1903.

A major point of interest is that the autopsy report lists the dead man's eyes as being brown. When Dillinger took a physical examination for the Navy on July 24, 1923, his eyes were described as being blue. On an FBI wanted poster issued by J. Edgar Hoover on March 12, 1934, the eyes were listed as gray. Why this inconsistency? The feeling of some Chicago reporters at the time the autopsy report was found was that the document was "lost" on orders from some superior when it was discovered that the wrong man had been killed. Others suggest that so many journalists called for the report immediately after Dillinger's death, that it was taken out of the file and kept readily accessible; it was misplaced from there.

A very different opinion comes from medical examiner Stein in an interview with two of the *Tribune*'s reporters, Ed Baumann and John O'Brien. The discrepancy in eye color, according to Stein, "doesn't mean a darn thing . . . after death there can be a clouding of the cornea, and you [could] have difficulty telling the color of the iris."

The rest of the autopsy report, although grizzly, progresses without contention: One bullet hit Dillinger in the back of the neck and passed through the right eye. Other bullet paths were noted, and the condition of his head, neck, chest, heart and abdomen are recorded, as well as the contents of Dillinger's last supper—red peppers, meat and vegetables.

Fact or Fiction?

It is absolutely amazing how many stories developed around Dillinger during and after the ten months of terror he inflicted on the nation. Perhaps it was because he rose so sharply to national prominence or because his exploits were so daring, or, maybe it was simply because his reign was so brief, Dillinger has surrounding his life (and death) innumerable myths and legends.

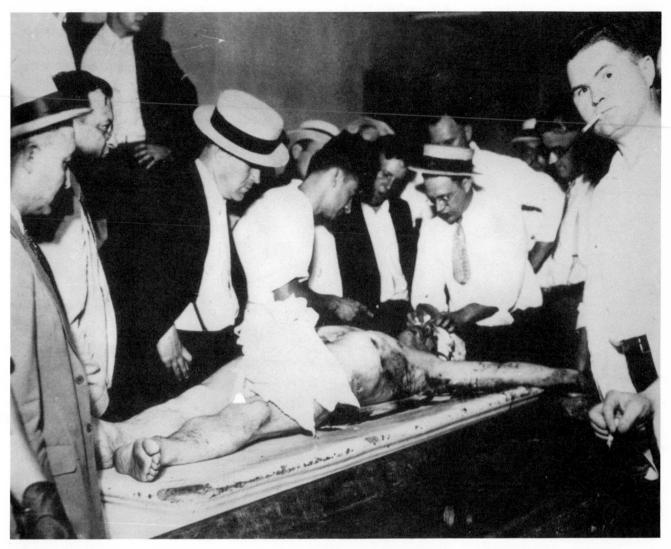

Was Dillinger at Little Bohemia?

Virgil Wrege, a guitar-playing masonry contractor from Lac du Flambeau, made the categorical statement: "He was never there that night."

Dillinger was on his way to Little Bohemia, that's true. But he was delayed when he spun his car into a ditch off Highway 13 in Mellen, Wisconsin, where my folks lived. My father helped pull his car out of the ditch. While the wrecker was on its way to help, Dillinger went to the nearby Mellen Plymouth garage and hot-wired a Plymouth. He then headed north to Ashland, and later down to Highway 51 to Little Bohemia. He was arriving there the night of the shoot-out (April 22, 1934) when he saw lawmen all over the place. He turned around and then escaped. But he was never at Little Bohemia.

Wrege's statement that Dillinger was never at Little Bohemia is new fuel to the mystery of Dillinger in the Northwoods. Many find

A carnival-like atmosphere erupted around the blood-soaked body of John Herbert Dillinger in the Cook County Morgue. Newspaper pictures at the time identified the man in the straw hat as the coroner, Dr. Charles D. Parker. Another report said he was actually a reporter for the Chicago *Tribune*. *National Archives' photo.*

Wrege's statement hard to believe. But then, there is a hint that Dillinger was not killed by federal agents on that hot night in Chicago near the Biograph Theater either. Author Jay Robert Nash claims it was a small-time hood named Jimmy Lawrence, who moved from Wisconsin to Chicago about 1930.

Wrege also went on to say, "Dillinger had a place next to Al Capone on Island Lake. It was where they relaxed. They were close to each other so they could have their guards eye each other. They were comfortable that way."

Dillinger's "Mything" Part?

There is not, and never was, an abnormally large part of Dillinger in the Smithsonian Institution—or anywhere else, for that matter.
—CHICAGO TRIBUNE, July 22, 1984

The Chicago *Tribune* carried a piece in its Sunday paper on July 22, 1984, concerning the myth of Dillinger's alleged humdinger of a penis. Rumors and stories of the gangster's giant member had been circulating for years. It seemed every time there was a slow week, the tabloids would start up the fun again. The *Tribune* set out to straighten the record. It succeeded only in adding fuel to the inferno.

Of course, using the word "penis" in a Sunday feature article was a little touchy. I remember the controversy over using it in reviews of Desmond Morris's *Naked Ape*. Morris didn't use euphemisms and the paper still did. Anyway, in the article on Dillinger,

Chicago *Daily News* paper of July 23, 1934, showing Dillinger in the county morgue. Note the strange bulge of the sheet. Surely whatever is making this is too high on Dillinger's torso to be any part of his anatomy. But rumors often need less to get started. When in later photos the "bulge" was gone, speculators believed it had been removed, pickled and sent to J. Edgar Hoover. *Tom Hollatz photo.*

the word "penis" was withheld until the jump page where the story got down to the nub of the mystery.

> . . . But perhaps the most persistent rumor, even asked by the FBI agents, concerns Dillinger's penis.
>
> "We get a couple of questions a month," said Katherine Neill, manager of telephone information service at the Smithsonian Institute. "Usually they say, 'Do you have anything that belongs to John Dillinger?' The party line here is that we have no anatomical parts belonging to John Dillinger in this museum."
>
> Dr. David Fisher of North Michigan Avenue, as an intern, assisted in the Dillinger autopsy. "I have no recollection of it being of an abnormal size," said Fisher. "I definitely would have noticed."
>
> The origin of the rumor perhaps may be found by looking at a photograph taken when Dillinger's body was on display at the morgue. Dillinger is pictured on the autopsy table, covered by a sheet from neck to ankles. A part of the table under the sheet may have been mistaken for a part of Dillinger.
>
> Fisher said, however, that Dillinger's heart and brain were removed. The heart was returned. The brain was preserved in a jar in case futher tests were needed. That jar has disappeared and probably was thrown out decades ago.

I contacted the FBI about the legend of Dillinger's giant penis. On July 12, 1984, I got this response:

> In response to your recent letter, I regret that you have been misled. Various rumors regarding John Dillinger have circulated for years, and the specimen 'in formaldehyde at the FBI' is one of them. One variation on this spurious claim is that it is maintained at Walter Reed Military Hospital.

However, the rumors persist of Dillinger's penis being preserved pickled in a jar in the J. Edgar Hoover FBI Building in Washington D.C. The thought seems to be that Hoover hated Dillinger to the tenth power after he eluded the Feds at Little Bohemia. Hoover was supposed to be so driven in his pursuit of Dillinger after that, that the "pound of flesh" he wanted at Dillinger's death was no figurative statement, but something very specific.

This rumor, as noted, took root in 1934, when the body of Dillinger was taken to the morgue for dissection by forensic pathologists. That member—reportedly 14 inches in flaccid state, 20 inches erect—was allegedly amputated by an overenthusiastic pathologist. It was in later years that reports of its being in the Smithsonian Institution surfaced. But there are some 65 million objects at the Smithsonian, and adjacent to it is the Medical Museum of the Armed Forces Institute of Pathology.

Tour guides, who are questioned daily about Dillinger's penis, think tourists wandered into that adjacent building thinking that they were still at the Smithsonian. The medical museum houses some pretty gruesome examples of diseased and oversized body parts, including penises and testes. There are also pictures of victims of gunshot wounds. According to the Smithsonian tour guides, it may have been in the medical museum that visitors saw something they believed was Dillinger's penis. The bizarre medical collection has since been moved to the Walter Reed Army Medical Center. Sources there claim Dillinger's organ has never been one of its displays.

Why is there such fascination with Dillinger's penis? Would it make a difference in history if it was as large as is claimed? Or if is wasn't? The other sexual rumor, of course, is that Dillinger and Baby Face Nelson had a homosexual relationship and that the many ladies they had in their company were only cover. Personally, it sounds like another slow news day's daydreams.

John Dillinger Buried $200,000 in the Northwoods

Did John Dillinger bury some $200,000 in a suitcase in Wisconsin's Northwoods? That's an unanswered question.

In *The People's Almanac No. 2* by David Wallenchinsky and Irving Wallace, the claim is made that in Dillinger's mysterious suitcase is one of the great unclaimed treasures of the world.

The money, it is alleged, was buried in the woods three months before Dillinger's death. So states author Ken Krippene in his book *Buried Treasure.* Krippene reportedly heard the story from Patricia Cherrington, one of the molls in Dillinger's gang.

When I told the story to Emil Wanatka Jr., owner of Little Bohemia, he said, "Nonsense . . . I have that old suitcase."

Krippene asserts, however, that Dillinger, on the night of April 22, 1934 (the night of his escape from Little Bohemia), ran to a spot where he buried the loot.

The $200,000 in that suitcase, Krippene claims, is in small bills, the cash from the sale of one million dollars in stolen securities. The fact that Dillinger had that cash is not denied. In their days of rage, Dillinger and his cohorts grabbed some $500,000.

I was searching through some old newspaper clippings in a broken down garage in Boulder Junction, Wisconsin, when I found an article. The clip was yellow and about ready to fall apart. There was no attribution, but it had to be from a local newspaper.

The headline read: EAGLE RIVER—WAS DILLINGER IN EAGLE RIVER?

The article went on to say:

> This is the question residents are asking themselves this week as they recall the mysterious arrival of four men, two of them negroes and two disguised as negroes, who stayed at a local rooming house. These men arrived Tuesday afternoon, March 27, shortly after the

Dillinger shooting escape from St. Paul, and left the next day.

All were dressed much alike and carried new luggage. Only one ate at the place where the group stayed. The one, which the owners of the rooming house now identify as having features like Dillinger, remained in his room the entire time of the stay and received his meals there. The others ate elsewhere, but were refused service at one of the local restaurants.

The men left Wednesday morning. As they were leaving, the owners of the lodging house became suspicious because the features of the two men were not at all negroid and closer investigation confirmed these suspicions. They immediately looked at the license plate as the men drove off. The license number was issued by the state of Missouri, and the number was 125-285. The car was a Ford sedan.

Tuesday evening a man entered Edgewater cottages and demanded liquor. A. J. Herbert refused to sell the liquor, and the man left. The car he came in was kept on the highway, and there were other men in it. Because of his roughness, they regarded him as a suspicious character.

If the four men described in this article were really Dillinger and his gang hiding out from the law, then it could have been that during that March 27th visit to Eagle River, just a few weeks before the escape from Little Bohemia, Dillinger could have stashed his loot.

Emil Wanatka debunks this story, but there are several who take the tales of buried treasure as truth . . . or an enticing possibility. Don Coan, a loquacious Northwoods tavern owner, recently purchased a metal detector to search for the lost loot. "Even it it's not there," Coan grins, "the challenge will be fun." But Don is noted for his optimism—"I've been a Cubs fan for years."

The Keys to Dillinger's Loot

The People's Almanac No. 2 lists the lost Dillinger loot among other tales of missing wealth, including the Lost Dutchman Mine, Joe Mullinene's Loot, Blackbeard's Treasure, Captain Kidd's Treasure, and others. But there are a lot of people out there who like to daydream about instant wealth. Readers' Digest and Publishers' Clearing House have capitalized on that dream for years. And it's never been proven that Dillinger *didn't* bury that suitcase of money in the Northwoods. And if he did . . .

There are three areas that deserve consideration from any who hold the dream of Dillinger's lost loot in his or her heart:

The Eagle River Area north of Land O'Lakes, Wisconsin to the Watersmeet, Michigan, area. Highway 45 is lined with possible spots. That's the problem: there are thousands of spots throughout those forests.

Woodruff to Manitowish Waters, Wisconsin, along the old Highway 51. That was the gang's main route when going to and from Little Bohemia. One possible key location could be at the northeastern corner of Highway H and Highway 51. There's an old airport there. Bert Warner, 85, of nearby Sayner, Wisconsin, remembers the date of the Dillinger invasion. "I had an airport here in Sayner, two runways—north and south and east and west. I was heading up to the airport . . . [when] I spotted a strange plane there. Then I spotted a man in a fedora and a big coat. He had something wrapped in a blanket. I caught a glimpse of it . . . it was a machine gun. The man looked mean. I said nothing, but turned and walked away. For some reason, I expected to be shot."

Manitowish Waters, Wisconsin, where Ken Krippene in *Buried Treasure* believes the cash is buried. He claims it is north of Little Bohemia "two pines and an oak." That clue isn't as good as it sounds as there are zillions of pines and oaks in the Northwoods. Even still, Manitowish Waters would be my first choice.

Whether Dillinger buried the $200,000 in a suitcase in the Northwoods or not is the question. If it is true, those old bills—mostly silver certificates—would bring in a not-so-small fortune from the collectors, not to mention the face value of the bills.

Look at it this way, you would probably have a better shot at finding Dillinger's lost loot than winning the lottery.

Did Dillinger Die at the Biograph? Dillinger's French Connection

When the tabloids got into the game of Dillinger hiding his loot, the "discoveries" instantly got more bizarre. The latest was that a fortune, reportedly belonging to Dillinger, was uncovered in a French resort where the "notorious bank robber spent the final years of his life." (Of course this assumes both that there actually was a fortune of hidden loot, and that Dillinger lived past that July night in 1934.)

The article goes on to make that claim that Dillinger was not gunned down near the Biograph Theater on July 22, 1934, that it was really Jimmy Lawrence who died. This is the same theory espoused by author Jay Robert Nash in his book *The Dillinger Dossier*.

One tabloid alleges: "There's over a million dollars here, and some of it in American cash dating back to the 1930s, says Pierre LeDoux, a French investigator who has been studying the loot."

Again, it should be pointed out that the source of this latest Dillinger "discovery" was a tabloid. Take it from there . . .

Dillinger's Girl—
Evelyn "Billie" Frechette

"God, she was beautiful!"

That's how a Columbus, Ohio, business executive described Evelyn "Billie" Frechette, the half-Indian girl who was John Dillinger's love.

Evelyn "Billie" Frechette, John Dillinger's beautiful girl. *FBI photo.*

The executive revealed that he had dated Billie after she was released from prison in the late 1930s for "obstruction of justice" in her attempts to hide Dillinger from the Feds.

The last time John Dillinger saw Billie was on April 9, 1934, when she was picked up by federal agents in Chicago in a bar at 416 North State Street. Dillinger had stood in the shadows just across the street and watched as FBI man Melvin Purvis and his men hauled her away.

As the car moved away, Dillinger lit a cigarette. Evelyn saw it and knew it was Dillinger, but said nothing.

Evelyn first met John Dillinger at the Chicago Exposition in 1933. She liked his athletic style as he moved with the grace of a smooth-fielding infielder, which he was. In several bank robberies, it is said Dillinger leaped over bank counters with the agility of a second baseman avoiding the attempted breakup of a doubleplay by a hard-sliding base runner.

On March 3, 1934, Frechette was in the Chicago office of Atty. Louis Piquett—Dillinger's attorney—seeking a divorce from Welton Sparks, a convicted convict serving time whom she had married before meeting Dillinger. She wanted the divorce so she could marry "Johnnie." That marriage never occurred. A month later she was arrested by the FBI, and while awaiting trail and her jail term, John Dillinger was killed by the Feds at the Biograph Theater.

After Dillinger's death on that hot, steamy Chicago night, Billie was said to have wept. She was twenty-seven at the time.

In 1945, in its in-house publication "The Investigator," the FBI went somewhat Hollywood in its description of the ties between Billie Frechette and John Dillinger.

> . . . romantic pictures [were painted] of the misguided youth and his . . . sweetheart, the half-breed Indian girl, Evelyn Frechette. Thousands of women sighed at the adventures of the dangerous duo and would have gladly exchanged places with Evelyn for just "one day in the sun." American youth chewed gum, adopted the Hollywood version of the underworld argot, and began to shift their adolescent hero-worship from "wild-western movie cowboys" to the notorious gunmen of the day . . . the pulse of the nation, stimulated by the shallow glamour and robust sensualities of those public enemies, quickened perceptibly over night, public opinion swayed to an alarming admiration for the cleverness of the Dillinger mob . . .

Billie Frechette received a two-year sentence and a $1,000 fine for obstruction of justice in her attempts to conceal from police and FBI agents the whereabouts of John Dillinger. This was served at Milan, Michigan.

In later years, Billie hit the bars, and hard. One who met her and was awed by her aging beauty was Jim "Durkee Spice King" Ford of Green Bay, Wisconsin. Ford, who as a teen knew many of the gangsters who flooded the Minocqua, Wisconsin, resort community of the 1930s, recalled that first meeting with Evelyn:

> It was in a bar near Shawano. I moved over near her to say hello. Out of the corner of my eye, I noticed what I'd call her chauffeur (or bodyguard) propped up in a chair against the wall. He just stared at me, but didn't say anything. I started chatting with her, bought her a drink. We talked about Dillinger only briefly, and about her career on the road with a carnival. She made her living talking to the public about Dillinger. Boy, one thing I remember is that she could really drink.
>
> Actually, it was kind of sad meeting her. Here was perhaps the most beautiful girl of the day sipping whiskey in a dimly-lit bar . . . from the headlines of the '30s, here Billie's life had come to the tragic reality of a scuzzy bar. Sad in a word.

When Dillinger was ambushed outside the Biograph Theater, some say he wasn't reaching for his gun. One of the newspapers claimed that Dillinger held a locket in his closed fist as he lay in his own blood in the darkened alley. In that locket was a picture of Billie.

Dillinger Mile Posts

1903 - Born in Mooresville, Indiana, rural village, the son of a highly respected family of Quaker stock.

1916 - Entered Mooresville high school and became a baseball star. Proficient in his studies.

1924 - Robbed an aged Mooresville merchant, Frank Morgan, of $550.00, slugging him on the street. Sentenced to a term of 10 to 20 years.

May, 1933 - Paroled from Indiana state prison at Michigan City and promptly went on a bank robbing spree.

September, 1933 - Ten convicts escape from Michigan City with guns smuggled to them by Dillinger . . . on the same day, Dillinger was jailed at Dayton, Ohio, for bank robbery, being transferred to jail at Lima, Ohio.

October 21, 1933 - Freed from Lima jail by fugitives he helped deliver from Michigan City. Sheriff Jess Sarber of Lima was killed.

January 15, 1934 - Killed Policeman William P. O'Malley while robbing an East Chicago, Indiana, bank of $23,000.00—one of a score of bank robberies that netted the gang $500,000.00 or more.

January 23, 1934 - Captured with Harry Pierpont, Charles Makley and Russell Clark, all since convicted for killing Sarber, at Tucson, Arizona.

January 28, 1934 - Jailed at Crown Point, Indiana, to await trial for killing O'Malley.

March 3, 1934 - Walked out of the Crown Point jail with a wooden gun, accompanied by Herbert Youngblood, Negro murderer later killed by police at Port Huron, Michigan.

March 31, 1934 - Fled from St. Paul, Minnesota, apartment in fusillade of bullets fired by police and government men.

In the next few weeks Dillinger was reported seen in dozens of places and was proved to have visited his father at Mooresville and to have spent time in St. Paul, Chicago and Sault Ste. Marie, Wis-

The fingerprints of John Dillinger taken while on the slab in the county morgue after he was gunned down by federal agents near the Biograph Theater in Chicago. *FBI photo.*

consin, "taking over" the place with a party of six men and three women.

April 22, 1934 - Jumped out a window of the Little Bohemia resort, escaping with six men, leaving two men killed and four wounded in his wake.

July 22, 1934 - Killed outside the Biograph Theater by government agents Cowley and Hollis.

Dillinger's Victims

October 21, 1933 - Sheriff Jess Sarber of Allen County, Ohio. Slain by Dillinger mobsters in freeing Dillinger from jail.

December 14, 1933 - Police Sgt. William T. Shanley killed in Chicago as John Hamilton, Dillinger lieutenant, escaped police trap.

December 20, 1933 - Patrolman Eugene Teague, Indiana state policeman. Slain in gun battle at Parks, Illinois, as Edward Shouse, member of Dillinger's gang, was captured.

December 21, 1933 - Three men slain by Chicago police as they sought Dillinger in North Side apartment. The three: Lewis Katzwitz, Streator, Illinois; Sam Ginsburg, escaped Michigan prisoner; and Charles Tilden, escaped Illinois prisoner.

January 6, 1934 - Jack Klutas, gang leader affiliated with Dillinger. Shot to death in the Chicago suburb of Bellwood by police hunting him and Dillinger. Walter Detrick, Dillinger gangster, captured.

Janaury 14, 1934 - Policeman William O'Malley of East Chicago, Indiana, slain by bank robbers. Dillinger was charged with this murder.

March 16, 1934 - Herbert Youngblood, Gary, Indiana, escaped with Dillinger from jail at Crown Point, Indiana. Youngblood was later killed at Port Huron, Michigan, in a gun battle with officers. Undersheriff Charles Cavanaugh was fatally wounded in that fight.

April 11, 1934 - Eugene Green, who fled with Dillinger from a St. Paul apartment March 31st, died from gunshot wounds inflicted when he was shot down three days later by government agents.

April 22, 1934 - W. Carter Baum, federal agent from Chicago, and Eugene Boiseneau of Mellen, Wisconsin—killed as Dillinger and six associates escaped from an elaborate police trap at the Little Bohemia resort near Mercer, Wisconsin. Four others were wounded.

Interview with Emil Wanatka Jr.

It was a raw and misting afternoon when I met with Emil Wanatka Jr., who was eight years old at the time when John Dillinger and his gang vacationed in the Northwoods that April weekend in 1934.

"It was here by this cabinet that Dillinger gave me a quarter," said Emil Wanatka Jr. *Tom Hollatz photo.*

TH: The FBI under young J. Edgar Hoover blundered what would have been a magnificent arrest and turned the FBI into a laughing stock, which almost killed that fledgling career.

Emil: I don't think you really can blame Hoover for that. Blame the man in charge, if you will—Melvin Purvis.

TH: I've heard that the number of lawmen who stalked Dillinger that night and then blew away the car with the CCC workers in it was anywhere from 15 to over 100. How many?

Emil: I guess it was something like 50 when you count the locals who were asked to help out.

TH: Actually, what do you remember about that time?

Emil: You must remember I was eight, and what does an eight-year-old really remember? But I do remember specific things. (In the large kitchen of Little Bohemia, Emil walked over to an old cabinet.) See this cabinet? I remember it had a mirror on it. John Dillinger was right here. I remember that he gave me a quarter to buy ice cream. Now a quarter was a lot of money in those days, mind you. He was nice to me. I remember that.

TH: What about Baby Face Nelson?

Emil: He was a very mean man. I'll never forget that. I quit playing baseball with him because he threw the ball too hard. It was a hard softball, if you will, but he fired it hard.

A cabin at Little Bohemia was turned into a museum, operated for a few years by Dillinger's father, John W. Dillinger, and the gangster's sister Audrey. *Little Bohemia Collection.*

One of the artifacts in the Dillinger museum at Little Bohemia is a tin can shot full of holes during a target-practice session on Saturday, April 21, 1934, by Dillinger gang members. *Tom Hollatz photo.*

TH: You have a can in the Dillinger museum filled with bullet holes. Where did they target practice?

Emil: Just east of the lodge, some 700 feet away. There was a pasture there then.

TH: In the books and articles I've read about the great escape, there seems to be some confusion as to where the Feds started shooting, eventually killing one of the CCC workers.

Emil: It was at the gate—the entrance (adjacent to Highway 51).

TH: Where were you when it all happened?

Emil: I was at Palmer Hanson's home on Spider Lake. On Saturday, April 21, Billy Hanson and I were at his house with Cal LaPorte, whose birthday it was. It was a sleep-over for two nights. The reason I got out is that my parents said it would look strange if I didn't make the birthday party.

TH: Where was your mom? Wasn't she out of Little Bohemia too?

Emil: My mother [Nancy Wanatka] was at Voss'. (She, Ruth Voss, George and Lloyd were brothers and sisters.)

TH: When did you find out about the shooting?

Emil: It was the day after. Palmer Hanson was driving us home and he said, "You had a shooting at Little Bohemia last night." It really didn't register on me as to what kind of shooting or anything like that.

TH: What about the Jay Robert Nash book *The Dillinger Dossier* which claims Dillinger lived after the Biograph shooting on July 22, 1934, and the Feds really killed Jimmy Lawrence.

Emil: I don't believe it and neither did the Dillinger family. Audrey [John Dillinger's sister] was here for a time, and her father worked here in the museum. When he was here we had the fake pistol Dillinger carved out of wood to escape from prison. Also the bloodied shirt he was murdered in. When he left, he took them with him. I believe they're in an Indiana museum now.

Adjacent to Little Bohemia is the John Dillinger museum. It was the cabin where Baby Face and his wife Helen Gillis stayed during the vacation escape to the Northwoods. When John Dillinger Sr. operated the museum, he and Emil's father were partners and split the profits.

In that museum, the curious can view John Dillinger's underwear, his dress shirts, the leather valise the gang reportedly carried

Emil Wanatka Jr. shows John Dillinger's escape route. On April 22, 1934, the winter's deep snow provided a safe cushion for Dillinger and his associates. *Tom Hollatz photo.*

"My father found this under Dillinger's bed," said Emil Wanatka Jr. Dillinger's rifle is a .351 Winchester self-loading piece that used smokeless cartridges. Five rounds were contained in a detachable box magazine. *Tom Hollatz photo.*

their loot in, dresses of their molls, a pickle can Baby Face Nelson and Dillinger used for target practice. There is the bed, complete with original chenille spread, where Dillinger slept. There are combs and brushes and even a tin of Dillinger's Ex-Lax tablets.

The museum also features two interesting letters that Dillinger wrote. In one, to a girlfriend, he strangely writes for her to love him, "even a little." The other letter was to his father in Indiana. He says, "I've been a disappointment to you . . . Dad, I'm not guilty of half of the things I'm charged with, and I've never hurt anyone."

Emil: I believe Dillinger killed one cop.

TH: Before your dad bought this place, he had a place in Chicago, didn't he?

Emil: He had a lot of interesting customers in Chicago. Many of them were "the boys" as they say. Then on one day three or four of his best customers were murdered. They were killed on February 14, 1929 in the St. Valentine's Day Massacre. That's when he decided to get out of the city and move to the Northwoods.

TH: When Dillinger and his gang fled that night, they left a lot of things behind. Tell me about the guns.

Emil: Here they are. (He displayed a .351 semi-automatic rifle left by Dillinger under his bed and the .45 Colt left by Baby Face.)

George "Baby Face" Nelson's .45 found by Emil Wanatka Sr. after the gangster fled Little Bohemia April 22, 1934. The serial number is C160461. The last "1" looks indented, as though altered. *Tom Hollatz photo.*

The FBI has asked me numerous times for them, but I still want them. I had the rifle blued, maybe I shouldn't have. (Emil cocked it.) This was a powerhouse. (He then removed Baby Face's .45 from its holster.) One of the most powerful weapons ever made. And the Army is changing them, doing away with it.

TH: What happened with your father and the Baby Face shooting incident?

Emil: It all happened at the Alvin Koerner home (on Spider Lake). My father was with Baby Face. Baby Face grabbed my dad and left some scared hostages in the Koerner home. Baby Face forced by father to drive, sitting next to him. The car choked, and Nelson became madder. Just then a car turned in from the highway. The car carried two FBI men and the local constable. When they couldn't move any further [the way blocked by the other car], Baby Face jumped out to confront the startled agents and Constable Christensen. That's when my father jumped out of the car and rolled over a high snowbank to get away. I guess he was gone after that for about four days. I think he hid in Lac de Flambeau.

It was then that Baby Face Nelson went berserk, smashing the front windshield. In the brutal havoc that followed, W. Carter Baum, an FBI agent, was killed, and Special Agent Jay Newman, a Mormon lay preacher, and Christensen were wounded in the bloodbath in the snow.

ARSENAL OF DILLINGER AND GANG

One of the most popular tourist features at FBI headquarters in Washington D.C. is Dillinger's arsenal. Shown is his death mask, a bullet-proof vest and the straw hat he was wearing the night he was killed, July 22, 1934, near the Biograph Theater in Chicago. *FBI photo.*

Tacked to a wall in the Dillinger Museum at Little Bohemia is a photo of John Dillinger, Sr., who hit the road to talk about his late son in theaters across the Midwest. Also appearing with John Sr. was his daughter Audrey. Later, both were hired by Emil Wanatka Sr. to talk to curious tourists about Dillinger's life. *Little Bohemia Collection.*

BABY FACE NELSON

Lester M. Gillis was a small man. At five feet four inches tall and 133 pounds, he may not have been the most imposing figure of a man, but he made up for his physical limitations by being mean and violent. Lester, alias Baby Face Nelson, was a minor actor in the Dillinger saga until after the flight from Little Bohemia. Then he became the leading villian.

When the bullets started exploding into the car of the CCC workers, Dillinger and Baby Face bailed out the back window of Little Bohemia. They split up almost immediately, Dillinger going north, and Nelson heading south along the shore of Little Star Lake. He stumbled through the thick underbrush and snow drifts in the dark for some forty minutes before he came upon the resort owned by Mr. and Mrs. G. W. Lang, an aged couple.

Nelson screamed at them to drive "south" down Highway 51, which would have taken them straight to the FBI staging area at Voss's Resort on Spider Lake. But Nelson turned off the car's headlights before the Highway 51 bridge and Voss's. He noticed a well-lighted house some 100 yards to the left. He and the Langs left the car and went up to the house.

Alvin Koerner was edgy that night after receiving two phone calls from Little Bohemia. He had been watching the highway and noticed the car Nelson had just abandoned. Quickly, Koerner called the Feds at Voss's and told them of the strange car with its headlights out.

As he hung up, Nelson and the Langs entered.

George LaPorte, brother of Mrs. Wanatka and Mrs. Ruth Voss

The entrance to Voss' Resort, the staging area for the Feds attempting to take Dillinger and the gang at Little Bohemia. Later that night, after escaping Little Bo, Baby Face Nelson saw the lights at Voss' and avoided it. *Tom Hollatz photo.*

of Voss's Resort, was also heading for Koerner's. He had refused to pick up a hitchhiker on the way (which later turned out to be Homer Van Meter, one of the fleeing Dillinger gang), but did stop to pick up Emil Wanatka Sr. and his two bartenders in their shirtsleeves, who also had run from the terror of Little Bohemia. LaPorte was driving to Koerner's to get coats for the three men.

LaPorte parked his Ford, and all four entered Koerner's. They were startled to see Baby Face Nelson holding his .45 on the Langs and Koerners. Suddenly, they, too, were hostages. The attempts both Wanatka and his bartender George Bazso made to get Nelson to put down his gun failed miserably. Instead, Baby Face grabbed Wanatka and Koerner as hostages. A terrified Mrs. Koerner screamed as they left. They piled into LaPorte's car, Nelson and Wanatka in the front seat. Then they began to ease down the drive.

Koerner's call to the FBI had not gone unanswered. Teams of agents and law enforcement personnel were being scattered all over the area hunting for the escaped criminals. At Koerner's call, a team of three men was sent to check out the car in front of Koerner's house. FBI agents Jay C. Newman of St. Paul, Minnesota, and W. Carter Baum, along with constable Carl Christensen, were dispatched. The men had seen the car and were proceeding up the Koerner drive. A car was just coming down the drive, but it stopped. A lone figure

Homer Van Meter, another of the Dillinger gang that escaped from Little Bohemia the night of April 22, 1934. *FBI photo.*

jumped out of the darkness and onto the running board of the agents' car. It was Baby Face Nelson.

The agents had their guns in their laps, but Nelson so surprised them that they did not have time to react before he stuck the barrel of his machine gun through the driver's window and started shooting. Baum was hit in the throat. Christensen and Newman flung open the doors and jumped from the car. Baum fell out of the car after them. Baum and Christensen ran some 40 feet to a fence where Baum collapsed and died, and Christensen lay unable to move any further, his body riddled by eight machine gun bullets.

After firing at Baum and Christensen, Baby Face Nelson turned his gun on Agent Newman, hitting him in the head. Newman fired back, however, but had little idea where he was aiming because of the blood that poured from his wound into his eyes. He gave that up, and crawled through the woods to a nearby resort where he telephoned for assistance.

At the same time that bullets were flying at the law enforcement people, Wanatka and Koerner weren't just spectating. The moment Baby Face left the car and opened fire on the agents, the two men dove from their vehicle. In the action, Wanatka claims Baby Face leveled some shots at him, but missed.

Baby Face Nelson took off in the agent's own car.

Help finally arrived for constable Christensen. He was taken 25

Here at the Alvin Koerner home in Manitowish Waters, shortly after eluding Feds at Little Bohemia, that Baby Face Nelson murdered Special Agent W. Carter Baum and wounded agent Jay Newman and Constable Carl Christensen. *Tom Hollatz photo.*

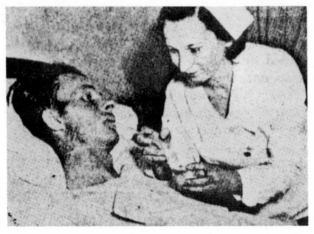

Constable Carl Christensen, recovering from his wounds after being shot by Baby Face Nelson as he fled the Wisconsin North-woods. *Camera/100 Collection.*

miles to the hospital in Ironwood, Michigan. Through the deep spring mud the trip took 2½ hours. It took Christensen 18 months to recover.

Meanwhile, Nelson was headed south on Highway 51 at 103 miles per hour in the FBI agents' car. After it became stuck on North Creek Road near Jag Lake, Baby Face walked through the woods to Lac du Flambeau Indian Reservation. It was now Monday morning, April 23rd.

Lac du Flambeau was a Chippewa Indian community where Baby Face Nelson hid out. *Photo Courtesy of Mike Aschenbrenner.*

Baby Face Nelson stayed three days with Ollie (Ole) Catfish, a Chippewa of the Lac du Flambeau, Wisconsin area, waiting for the heat to die down so he could escape the Feds. *Photo Courtesy of Mike Aschenbrenner.*

By late afternoon, Baby Face came to a small frame shack owned by a full-blooded Chippewa, Ollie (Ole) Catfish. Catfish, who was in his sixties, was building a fire to make maple sugar when Nelson came up to him.

Nelson told him to put out the fire. When Catfish balked, Nelson produced a gun. The fire—which might have attracted the Feds to that lonely cabin—was put out.

Nelson stayed with Catfish and his family for three nights. Then the two men walked along the old railroad bed to the town of Lac du Flambeau. They spotted the car of Adolph Goetz, a Merrill letter carrier, who was fishing for suckers at a nearby lake. Flashing his gun, Nelson took the startled mailman's keys and took the car.

The car broke down, but Nelson was now about 140 miles from

Little Bohemia. Posing as a CCC worker, Nelson got a farmer to drive him to Marshfield, Wisconsin for $20.00. When questioned later, the farmer thought Nelson was maybe 16 years old.

In Marshfield, Nelson went to the Marshfield Hardware and Auto Company where he purchased a 1929 Chevrolet.

In the days that followed, like Dillinger, Baby Face was spotted everywhere. There were reports of gun fights, car windows being sprayed by machine gun fire and autos being traced down empty roads. In Solon Springs, Wisconsin, a George Johnson, 40, was wounded when he attempted to stop a speeding car, thinking it contained Nelson. As one of the special deputies on the Dillinger-Nelson manhunt, he pursued the suspect car only to be injured from flying glass when his car was sprayed with bullets by those he pursued.

Nelson, however, was not captured in Wisconsin that April, nor officially seen in Wisconsin again.

The Bloody Highway Shootout

It was on November 27, 1934 that Inspector Samuel P. Cowley of the FBI's Chicago office received word that Nelson had been seen driving a stolen car. Two special agents spotted the vehicle near Barrington, Illinois. It was stalled. The vehicle contained longtime Nelson pal, John Paul Chase, and Nelson's wife, Helen Gillis (who had been at Little Bohemia).

Cowley scrambled to a nearby ditch with a submachine gun and the second FBI man, agent Herman Hollis, armed with a shotgun, crouched behind the FBI car.

Nelson opened up with his submachine gun, and Chase started firing his automatic rifle. Helen ran for cover, as did several nearby construction workers. After several exchanges, it appeared to be a stand-off.

One of the construction workers said at that point Nelson said, "I'm going down there and get those sons of bitches."

As Baby Face Nelson advanced on the FBI men, Cowley fired from his place in the ditch. Baby Face took a bullet in his side while he still walked forward. Another rat-a-tat-tat from Nelson's submachine gun almost cut Cowley in half. Then Nelson turned his weapon on Hollis, who dropped his empty shot gun and ran for cover behind a nearby telephone pole. Blasting away with a pistol, Hollis scored several hits on Baby Face before taking a fatal bullet to his head.

In the battle, Nelson had absorbed some 17 bullets. He staggered to the FBI car where Chase and Helen joined him. Chase was driving when they drove off.

It was the next day before Nelson's body was found, some 20 miles from the scene of one of the bloodiest bullet baths in gangster

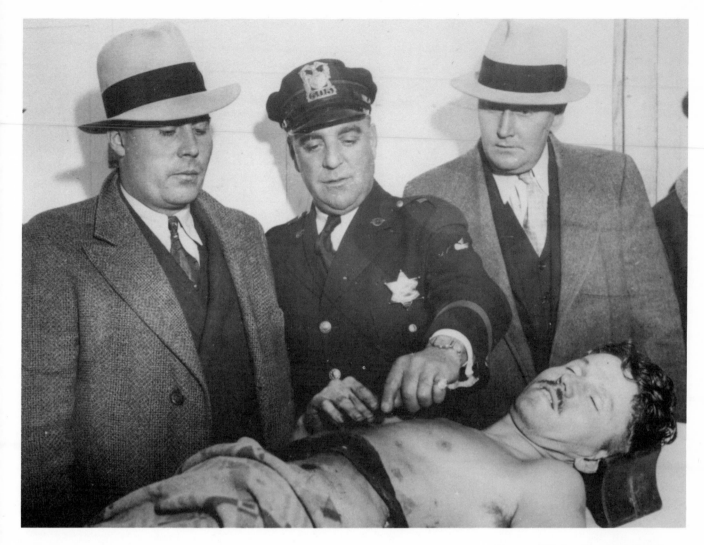

history. Nelson's body was stripped naked to slow identification. The seventeen bullet holes were a clue.

As for Chase, he died of cancer October 5, 1973. Helen Wawzynak, whom Baby Face met in 1929, was arrested on November 29, 1934. She served one year in the Women's Federal Reformatory in Milan, Michigan. Her later years were spent in the Chicago area.

George "Baby Face" Nelson's bullet-riddled body lies on an undertaker's slab in Niles, Illinois, November 27, 1934 after being found in a nearby ditch. Nelson, the former Lester Gillis, was mortally wounded in a savage gun battle with federal agents Sam Cowley and Herman Hollis. Hollis and Cowley were killed in the exchange. *AP/Wide World photo.*

1 9 2 0
2 1 ½ m.
2 7
4 8

"BIG AL" CAPONE

The Medill School of Journalism in 1930 polled its students as to whom they considered the year's ten outstanding personages in the world . . . the people who actually made history. Along with renown individuals such as Albert Einstein and Henry Ford, the students listed Alphonse Capone. There were two historical events which allowed a gangster to rise to such prominence in people's minds: the Volstead Act and the Great Depression.

On January 17, 1920, the Volstead Act was put into law. Al Capone turned twenty-one on that day too. What a birthday present. Just at a time when he was looking for his life's work, the government of the United States just about clobbers him over the head with work to do. If the government was going to make alcohol illegal, and if the population still wanted it, or could be enticed to want it, he would have all he could do to fill the need.

When enacted, there were only 1,520 Prohibition agents on the job trying to enforce dryness. They made a weekly salary of about $35—no highly paid jobs here. At the same time, it is said that Big Al made over $60 million in his life of undermining that law and getting around the enforcers. While many of the Prohibition agents were trying to function on a shoestring, Al was always a step or two ahead of them because he had the resources to do it. He could also afford to put lots of distance between himself and the men who actually "did the dirty work" of his business.

He may have started with bootlegging, but Big Al had dreams

Photo courtesy the FBI.

67

of greatness that transcended that "trucking" business. The gangster branched out into gambling with slot machines and roadhouses that paid him his due. He saw prostitution as just about the same kind of thing as booze: something that the people wanted but were told they couldn't have. But Big Al would give that to them too . . . for a price. He took advantage of the need people had, not necessarily only for booze and women, but just for some small excitement, some joy in their otherwise dreary lives. It may have been a once-in-a-lifetime event for some folks to sit in a speakeasy with their hearts thumping at the thought that the police could raid the place. It was better than a ride in an amusement park, more real than the flick on the silver screen.

The first clue that the thirst for booze was a marketable item came 59 minutes after the Volstead Act was put into law. At just about 1:00 a.m. on January 17, 1920, in Chicago, six masked and armed men invaded a railroad switching yard and bound two trainmen and also imprisoned six others in a shanty. The masked men then hit two freights grabbing crates of whiskey labeled "for medicinal purposes only." It was valued at some $100,000, but would sell for three times that on the streets.

"You can get much further with a kind word and a gun than you can get with a kind word alone."

AL CAPONE

Big Al's Charity

There is no doubt that Al Capone was a gangster, a bootlegger, a criminal of great notoriety, but during the time when public funds were drying up (even if the whiskey wasn't), and tax bills to assist the millions who were out of work and starving were drawing protests from the struggling public and the wealthy, Al Capone stepped in to lend a hand.

Capone's charity included a soup kitchen on the South Side of Chicago. The sign outside read: Free Food for the Workless. In a six-week period, Capone provided 120,000 meals at a cost of twelve thousand dollars. On Thanksgiving, Al gave away 5,000 turkeys. For Christmas, Capone tossed a big party for the poor in Chicago's Little Italy. John Kobler, in his book *Capone: The Life and World of Al Capone*, reported that during the festivities, an old woman knelt before him and kissed his hand.

While Judge John H. Lyle was proclaiming that Big Al deserved to die for his racketeering and bootlegging activities, many people were cheering him wherever he went. Once, at a Charlestown, Indiana, racetrack, thousands gave Capone a standing ovation when he appeared with his bodyguards. He clasped hands and reportedly walked through the race fans with his hands above his head. During a football game at Dyche Stadium, a gaggle of Boy Scouts cheered,

Al Capone. *National Archives'
photo.*

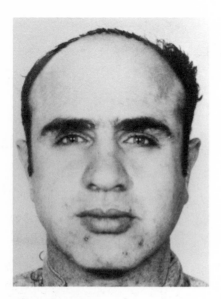

Big Al Capone. *FBI photo.*

"Yea, Al!" He had supplied them with tickets.

This was the stuff folk heroes were made of, a true Robin Hood in every sense. Al Capone, in the public eye, was a gangster. True enough. But he also helped people.

Al Capone even spoke of himself in those terms:

> I'm a public benefactor. . . . You can't cure thirst by law. They call Capone a bootlegger. Yes. It's bootleg while it's on the trucks, but when your host at the club, in the locker room or on the Gold Coast hands it to you on a silver platter, it's hospitality. What's Al done, then? He's supplied a legitimate demand. Some call it bootlegging. Some call it racketeering. I call it a business. They say I violate the prohibition law. Who doesn't?

Al Capone's Hideout

Like other gangsters of the era, Al Capone also enjoyed escaping Chicago's heat by heading up to the Northwoods. Near Couderay, Wisconsin, he made a place for himself and his gang when the need to get away from it all struck him. He was blatant enough about what he was doing when he built his cabin to call it "The Hideout." That place still exists and is owned and operated by Jean Houston, a former Chicagoan.

I visited her and The Hideout off Highway 70 and Highway CC. When I got there, she and her son Guy were installing an air-condi-

Al Capone's "Hideout" in Couderay, Wisconsin. *Tom Hollatz photo.*

The gift shop at the Hideout is Capone's former garage. Those black boxes on a line high in the wall hide portholes for machine guns. *Tom Hollatz photo.*

tioning unit in the dining room/bar area which had formerly been Capone's garage.

"Those are holes for machine guns," Jean said, pointing to the openings high on the stone wall.

Outside the gift shop is a beefy cartoon-like character holding a submachine gun. The shop itself features photos of Capone playing tennis, at a Cubs ball game meeting Stan Hack, and with various other celebrities.

"An old man came in here one day," Jean said, "and he said Capone was a saint." He said Al Capone took care of him for nine months, feeding his family during the Depression. It was like a mission for the gentleman to come here and look at Al's place.

We walked outside as it began to drizzle. Jean pointed at the fieldstone machine gun turret to the right, conveniently overlooking the entrance road. West of the lodge was Capone's jail.

"I don't know who Capone kept here," Jean said, "but it is a

The machine gun turret (on the hill at the left) faces the driveway and offers protection against the sudden invasion of an enemy gang or the FBI. *Tom Hollatz photo.*

strange place."

Inside the fieldstone structure was a table with two plastic skulls. The door was heavy and the window barred. In the back was an exercise yard.

We walked toward the main house, passing a swing that overlooked Cranberry Lake on the 400-acre estate.

"During Prohibition, planes carrying booze from Canada [which did not have a prohibition law] would land here. The gang would then take the booze to Chicago."

A trip through Al's holiday home turned out to be very interesting. Bear rugs and a plethora of antiques colored the porch, which featured a glass-encased bullet-proof vest. It was good looking, and fit naturally into a dark three-piece suit. The vest weighed some 25 pounds.

In the living room, I stopped to admire the rustic Northwoods beauty. Seemingly out of place were the stained glass windows high

The fieldstone jail on Al Capone's Hideout in Couderay, Wisconsin. *Tom Hollatz photo.*

on the east and west walls that captured the beginning and end of those long Northwoods summer days. Today, even in an overcast, they glowed.

There were wooden spiral staircases to the upper level bedrooms. Al's bedroom was in the northwest corner, overlooking the lake and the main roadway. A large rolltop desk and a poker table were on the north wall; a record of his favorite Caruso was on the old Victrola.

Downstairs, to the right of the fireplace I was startled by a figure behind the glass doors of the dining room.

"That does startle some people," Jean laughed. It was a mannequin dressed rather nattily. The figure had a large scar on the left side of its face. It was a haunting image of Al Capone to say the least.

The small cell inside the jail. *Tom Hollatz photo.*

The bar of the resort featured the drinks that made the '20s roar: "Between the Sheets, "Bee's Knees," "Bizzy Izzy," and the "Mary Pickford." There were also mugs, T-shirts, hats and other souvenirs for sale.

"When we moved here we didn't plan to make it a tourist attraction. People kept coming through the woods, pestering us," Jean said. "It was then we decided to open up to the public."

Guy (Jean's son) added, "People come from all over the world. Take this cigar. A box of Al Capone cigars was sent to me by a man who visited here from Germany. The 'Al Capone' is a popular cigar in Germany. And we get visitors from Italy. They know all about Al

It was almost real looking into
the 1925 dining room and seeing
this mannequin of Scareface toast-
ing a friend or a soon-to-die
enemy. *Tom Hollatz photo.*

Al Capone's swing overlooking Cranberry Lake where planes from Canada during Prohibition brought in illegal booze that the Capone mob then delivered to Chicago. *Tom Hollatz photo.*

in Italy. You know, if Al were alive today, I think he'd get a kick out of the place."

"We also get lots of visitors from Japan," Jean said. "Really, people think of Capone as a folk hero of sorts."

That folk image took root even as early as 1930 when Pasley's book on Al Capone was featured on the list of new books. In it, Capone was imaged as a "self-made man."

It was a success story—the tale of a young man who battled his way upward against great odds in the big city, determined to carve out a career for himself. The review of the book states: "His 'human' side thus revealed, the Chicago gang leader emerges as an Alger-like figure . . . Capone's career is unfolded in elaborate detail from the time when, as an obscure hoodlum of the Five Points gang of New York, he journeyed westward to seek his fortune. In the end he is seen basking in the sunshine . . . having lived to the age of 32—far past the life expectancy of the average gang leader."

The Florida Connection

A man with the wealth and advantages (not to mention legal difficulties) that Al Capone had, made it mandatory to have more than one "hideout." Besides his place in Couderay, Wisconsin, another place Al Capone loved was Florida. He had a beach bungalow there, as well as the top floor of the nine-story Hotel Ponce de Leon in downtown Miami. And, although the local government officials were outraged by the presence of the underworld king, they soon were swayed by his money. The economy of southern Florida was crashing, compounded by the 1926 hurricane which caused an estimated $100,000,000.00 in property damage and left 50,000 people homeless. Here, as he had done in Chicago, Al Capone began to spread his money around, creating an outward image of generosity and altruism. That image covered up some very unsavory traits.

The St. Valentine's Day Massacre

George "Bugs" Moran and his gang were rivals of Al Capone's gang in Chicago. They maintained headquarters at the S.M.C. Cartage Company or Hayer's Garage at 2122 North Clark Street, Chicago. On February 14, 1929, while Big Al was relaxing in his Florida comfort, well beyond any possibility of direct involvement, seven members of the Bugs Moran gang were cut down. The victims were Pete and Frank Gusenberg, safeblower John May, speakeasy proprietor and bank-robbery suspect James Clark, Adam Heyer, optometrist Dr. Reinhardt H. Schwimmer (who was just starting to play around with the mobsters) and Weinshank. All were cut down by the rapid fire of the tommy gun, the "Chicago piano."

The suspected principal gunman in the massacre was one of Capone's best triggers "Machine Gun" Jack McGurn. It was never proven. But if McGurn was not there, the Chicago police were sure he was not far from the action. And McGurn was devoted to Big Al.

If the police could not make a case to convict either McGurn (let alone Capone) in the St. Valentine's Day Massacre, other mobsters were not restricted by legalities. They were bitching—but not too loudly—that Al was giving the gangsters a "bad name." The St. Valentine's Day Massacre was just too much.

At a dinner, supposedly in honor of the acquittal of John Scalisi, Albert Anselmi and Hot Toad Joseph Guinta, all underworld thugs, Capone confronted the released men and threw wine in their faces. He accused them of trying to get control of the mob.

In the brutal attack that followed, Capone grabbed a baseball bat and beat all three men on their heads. When they collapsed to the floor, Capone continued to pound them. Then they were knifed and shot.

"This is virgin territory for whorehouses."

AL CAPONE

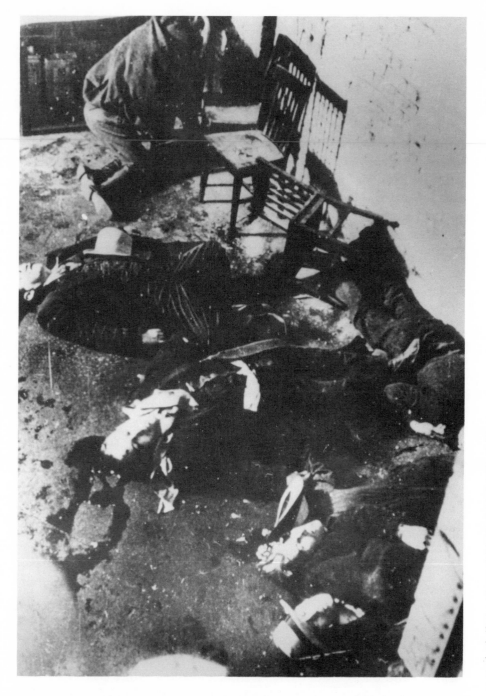

"Nobody shot me."

Last words of Frank Gusenberg, when asked by police who had shot him 14 times with a machine gun in the St. Valentine's Day massacre.

Six of the seven victims of the St. Valentine's Day Massacre lie in warm puddles of their own blood in the grease-smelly garage at 2122 North Clark Street in Chicago. The seventh, Frank Gusenberg, alias "Hock," lived for three hours with 14 bullets in him. He refused to tell who did the infamous deed on that bleak February 14th, 1929. Meanwhile, Al Capone, the architect of the slayings, was on a Florida vacation at his Palm Island estate—the perfect alibi. *AP/Wide World photo.*

The bludgeoned bodies of Guinta, Scalisi and Anselmi were found near the Indiana state line. Dr. Francis McNamara, thirty years a county jail physician, said that the punishment inflicted on the trio was unparalleled in his experience.

There was a nationwide grumbling by the mobsters. The savageness of the Capone attack and the St. Valentine's Day Massacre were too barbaric even for them. For the first time, Capone was seen in his true light. No one—not even his friends—were safe. Was this the same altruistic man who gave tickets to Boy Scouts and ran a soup line? Even for the sake of his generous pocketbook, a man like this could not be allowed to go unpunished. This was when the FBI succeeded in making their income tax evasion charge stick.

The Government Steps In

Something had to be done about Al Capone, but he was as slippery as an eel. He never seemed to be around when wicked deeds were being done. It would have been great to get him on a murder charge and lock him up forever, but that just wasn't going to happen. He stayed out of town when his hit men did their work, and other mobsters were now terrified to talk about anything relating to Al Capone, let alone testify against him in court.

But the federal government found a way to deal with Al Capone, that was creative and unexpected (as far as the gangsters were concerned). Al's income was estimated and a tax made due. That's how Big Al fell: income tax evasion.

At the peak of his career, Capone was making some $6 million a week, according to J. Edgar Hoover. In an effort to stop this archcriminal's activities, the government figured Al Capone's provable income and then determined the tax amounts due. The amounts due seemed paltry, but it was enough to put the man in prison.

Year	Income	Tax Due
1924	$123,101.89	$32,489.24
1925	$257,285.98	$55,365.25
1926	$195,676.00	$39,962.75
1927	$218,057.04	$45,557.76
1928	$140,535.93	$25,887.72
1929	$103,999.00	$15,817.76

"Let the worthy citizens of Chicago get their liquor the best way they can. I'm sick of the job. It's a thankless one and full of grief."

AL CAPONE

The Naples-born underworld boss, who had parlayed a fourth-grade education into a multi-million dollar career of gambling, bootlegging, prostitution, and racketeering, was being taken out of circulation for income tax evasion. On October 24, 1931, Capone was convicted of this crime and given eleven years in jail and $80,000 in fines and court costs by U.S. District Court Judge James H. Wilkerson. Al's request for bail pending appeal was denied. Of this sentence, Al Capone served eight years in Alcatraz.

He was released on November 19, 1939. But instead of going back into business, Al Capone became the victim of the same corruption that he had given the American public. Al Capone was a victim of syphilis. By the time he left prison, his mind had been affected to the point that he no longer was functional as an underworld leader. He succumbed to the disease a little over seven years later, dying on January 25, 1947.

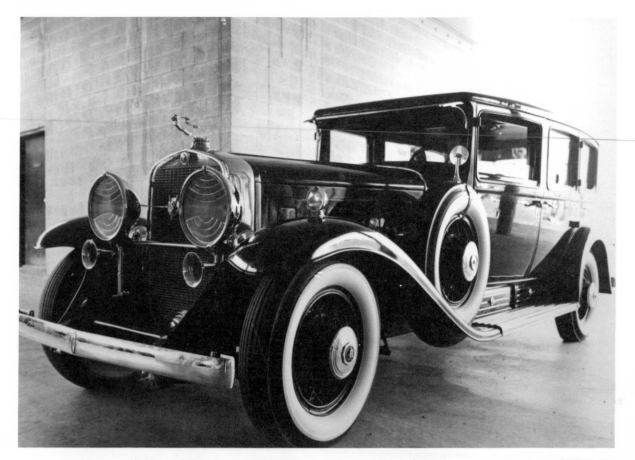

Two views of Al Capone's car. Found at the Imperial Palace Hotel & Casino, Las Vegas, there are some 200 antique cars in the collection. *Photos courtesy the Las Vegas News Bureau.*

RALPH CAPONE

The saga of Ralph "Bottles" Capone in the Northwoods is a disturbing one. There is a certain euphoria at the mere mention of his name, especially by those who knew him.

"Greatest human being I ever met . . ."

"He helped my family out . . ."

"He had a big heart . . . always loved to help out . . ."

The accolades are so numerous, you'd think old "Bottles" pushed nothing stronger than soda pop instead of booze in his Chicago gangster days. In the book *Northwoods Nostalgia*, Joyce Laabs paints a saintly picture of the man. Strange image for a gangster.

Ralph James Capone was born on January 12, 1894, to Gabriel and Teresa Capone of Naples, Italy. In 1922, Ralph followed his younger brother Al to Chicago. The next year the whole family moved out.

During Prohibition, Ralph sold beer as director of liquor sales for the mob. The FBI said that Ralph operated Waukesha Waters and also engaged in the wholesale distribution of beer. Waukesha Waters handled the distribution of mineral water from Waukesha Springs. This water went to restaurants, hotels and inns; in reality he sold beer to speakeasies. He also was a broker for cigarettes under the name of the Suburban Cigarette Service. On the side he engaged in bookmaking operations.

In the heyday of the Capone era in Chicago, Ralph was the cashier for the mob. The FBI claims Big Al was making some $6

Photo courtesy the FBI.

81

million a week during those peak years. Not a bad time to be a cashier.

Like his brother Al, Ralph Capone was charged with income tax evasion. According to veteran Chicago newsman Ray Brennan:

> Among the hoodlums so pestered [by Arthur P. Madden of the office of Internal Revenue] had been Capone's older and not-so-smart brother, Ralph. He was called "Bottles" because he supplied speakeasies with ginger ale and fizz water for mixed drinks.
>
> After about six months of harassment, Ralph testily conceded that he had had an income of $7,500 in 1923, another $7,500 in 1924, $20,000 in 1925 and $20,000 in 1926, for a total of $55,000. The tax agent filled out the usual forms for him, and Ralph—the chump—signed his name. The amount due in those days of dainty tax bites, was only $4,065.
>
> The payment would have been a pittance to him, since he customarily carried $10,000 in his pants pocket for "fall money," in case of an arrest, but he stalled on paying. He offered $1,000 in settlement, but Madden refused to accept it. The case dragged along, and the Government threatened to seize his racing stables of four horses.
>
> Ralph finally increased his offer to $2,500, but insisted he was broke and would have to borrow money. Again he signed a statement that he had no assets. Finally, he agreed to pay the entire $4,065, but he balked when told he would have to come up with $1,100 in penalties.
>
> If he had paid off, the history of the Capones might have had a far, far different ending.
>
> A widely-believed myth at the time was that President Hoover first set out to throttle [Al] Capone after the gangster annoyed him with a wild party at the Palm Island estate when the presidential yacht *Mayflower* was anchored nearby in Biscayne Bay. What really happened was that Frank Loesch got an audience with Mr. Hoover and convinced him that Al was a national disgrace and no longer could be tolerated.
>
> . . . Treasury agents tagged Bottles one evening as he walked down the aisle in the Chicago Stadium toward his ringside prize-fight seat. He was taken posthaste to the U.S. Courthouse and hidden away in a secluded office before the Syndicate's lawyers and bondsmen could spring him by a court writ or on bail.

Ralph finally admitted that a suburban bank balance of $25,237 was his, and he was not destitute as claimed. He was the first gangster to be caught on such charges, but was followed soon after by the conviction of his brother Al.

Ralph's prison term lasted from November 7, 1931 to February 27, 1934. He was let out early for good behavior.

The Move to the Northwoods

It was in the early 1940s that Ralph Capone and his wife purchased the Rex Hotel in Mercer, Wisconsin, for $65,000. The tavern

The FBI reported that in 1945 Ralph Capone purchased the Rex Hotel in Mercer, Wisconsin, for some $65,000. The tavern part of the hotel was known as Billy's Bar. Capone also owned Recap Lodge located at Martha Lake in Mercer. He was reported, according to the FBI, to have an interest in the Beaver Lodge, also in Mercer. *Tom Hollatz photo.*

part of the hotel was known as Billy's Bar. He also owned the Recap Lodge at Martha Lake in Mercer. It was also reported that he had at least an interest in Beaver Lodge in Mercer. He ran slot machines in these places and other establishments in the area; his alleged partner was Jack "Greasy Thumb" Guzik, supposed to be one of the heads of the Chicago gambling syndicate. For some 40 years until his death, Ralph and Madeleine lived in the Mercer area. They enjoyed the Northwoods and were visitors at Little Bohemia, the rustic Northwoods lodge made famous by John Dillinger and George "Baby Face" Nelson.

In the wilds of the Northwoods, Ralph enjoyed hunting for grouse and other birds. He also enjoyed trips to Canada for moose. He was an avid golfer, had a passion for baseball and played gin and pinochle. He also frequented Minocqua's Belle Isle and placed bets via the wire there to the tracks. And, he helped out his neighbors:

EMIL WANATKA, JR.: He wasn't a saint, but he was a good guy. The people here really loved him. If a home burned down, he was always first to start a fundraiser to help out. I'm not kidding. If someone needed a handout, Ralph would help. If you needed a bag of groceries, Ralph would help. He was a member of the Lions' Club, too. People don't understand that. I'll go on record and say he was one of the finest people I've ever met.

Ralph Capone relaxing at his home in Mercer, Wisconsin. *FBI photo.*

JIM FORD: Ralph was a great Green Bay Packer fan. He'd always get to the stadium two minutes before each game. Larry Fell [founded UPS], who was only a friend and not involved in the rackets, helped get him tickets. Once I sent him a team photo of the Packers in care of "Ralph Capone, Mercer, WI." The next time Ralph saw me, he said, "Please, just say 'Ralph, Mercer, WI.' I'll get it."

RICHARD GARVEY OF CUSTOM TREE SERVICE, MERCER: I worked as a bartender for Ralph. He was always great to me. He truly helped hundreds of people. The story is he helped many people who were losing their homes to the bankers. . . . When I worked there I also spotted many of the "boys" at the bar. Saw their shoulder holsters inside of their jackets. I learned never to ask any questions . . . you asked me if I ever heard someone say something rotten about Ralph. The answer is no. He was always there to help anyone . . .

Everywhere, it seems, there were glowing stories of Ralph's kindness and generosity. There are tales of his fighting a forest fire, shedding tears after shooting a troublesome bear and taking people in need into his home. And every bit of this may just well have happened. In a lot of ways Ralph Capone was a "great guy." But a conversation with Larry Bosacki, owner of Bosacki's Bar, may have revealed a reason for this. When asked why not one person in the Northwoods ever said a discouraging word about Ralph Capone, Larry started to laugh. "That's because a bird never craps in his own nest."

Ralph Capone, at the age of 81, died in November 1974 after several years of illness.

The living room of the Ralph Capone home in Mercer, Wisconsin. *FBI photo.*

The original log building which Madeliene (Hobbs) Capone operated for four years. *FBI photo.*

JOHN HENRY SEADLUND

"The World's Most Vicious Criminal"

Dillinger, as we all know, was "Public Enemy No. 1," attaining that rating on June 22, 1934, by J. Edgar Hoover. He was the most vicious, right? He had to be with that No. 1 designation. Or so I thought.

A friend with the FBI sparked my interest when he told me to check an old-old issue of "True Detective" with the story "How G-Men Captured Seadlund, the World's Most Vicious Criminal."

Seadlund? Who was Seadlund? I had researched every criminal —or so I thought—and never once drifted across the name of Seadlund—John Henry Seadlund. Even my favorite crime reader "The Encyclopedia of American Crime" by Carl Sifakis had no mention of Seadlund.

I found a well-worn copy of that vintage "True Detective" and the article by John Clement, special investigator for the magazine.

Clement, in a wonderfully tacky literary style, pictures Seadlund, 24, as a whiskey-guzzling, untrustworthy loafer in the iron-mining community of Ironton, Minnesota. "He had not worked in six years and his attitude showed plainly that he didn't intend to."

His life changed in the last week of March, 1934 when a green coupe "caked with mud slid to a curb." The "Joe Boyle from St. Paul" wanted Seadlund, who loved to hunt and fish, to find him a remote cabin in the woods where he could relax.

J. Edgar Hoover mugs it for the camera with an equally determined-looking boxer. It was Hoover who branded John Henry Seadlund as "America's Most Vicious Criminal." *FBI photo.*

Opposite Page: Spread from an old "True Detective," which told the story of John Henry Seadlund, the World's Most Vicious Criminal.

Seadlund soon discovered that "Mr. Boyle" was really Tommy Carroll, veteran bank robber and a member of "Dillinger's gang of killers." He had recently escaped from St. Paul police after being located in an apartment in Dayton's Bluff section.

From that chance encounter, the magazine related, J. Edgar Hoover, a few years later, would say of Seadlund: "He is the most vicious criminal in America today."

An item in a St. Paul newspaper gave Seadlund the idea for a crime. He noted in a dispatch from Chicago that Mayor Edward J. Kelly of Chicago was spending the weekend in his summer home in Eagle River, Wisconsin. Kelly's presence in Eagle River triggered an idea. Other wealthy Chicagoans vacationed there. Kidnapping and the following ransom could be one way to achieve big bucks. Meanwhile, he eyed the bank in Eagle River and the Minocqua bank located in another resort community nearby.

(*Top*) John Henry Seadlund (*left*) was a willing pupil of Tommy Carroll (*center*). James Atwood Gray (*above*), accomplice of Seadlund

(*Oval*) Young and attractive Mrs. 'Olive Borcia knew the terror that comes to a kidnap victim when she was snatched from the company of her husband, a Chicago night club operator, shortly before Seadlund and Gray committed the shocking crime that spelled doom

Joe DiMaggio (*left center*), slugging member of the New York Yankees, and "Dizzy" Dean (*above*), then a pitcher for the St. Louis Cardinals, were on Seadlund's preferred list for future kidnapings. (*Left*) The wilderness crypt, near Spooner, Wisconsin, where the notorious outlaw prepared to hide his victims

The Great Baseball Kidnapping Scam

Seadlund teamed up with James Atwood Gray. It was Gray who had what he thought was the most brilliant kidnapping idea of all time: "Kidnappin' big league baseball players!" Seadlund was enthusiastic about the younger Gray's idea.

Think of the money the ball club owners would pay to ransom back their star players! The St. Louis Cardinals would give a quarter of a million bucks if Dizzy Dean were snatched! Think what Jake Ruppert of the New York Yankees would shell out for one of his star sluggers—Lou Gehrig or Joe DiMaggio!

The two men sat and made plans for several hours. Dean, Gehrig or DiMaggio would be the best prospects for kidnapping, they agreed. Seadlund worked out the details. They would go to Chicago and wait until the Cards played the Cubs at Wrigley Field or the Yankees met the White Sox in Comiskey Park.

"We'll get a list of near relatives of DiMaggio, Gehrig and Dean," Seadlund said. "Then we'll get a policeman's uniform and go out to the ball-grounds. I'll wear the uniform, and after the game is over I'll go to the players' dressing room. I'll get the player we want and tell him that a relative—a brother or sister or cousin—had been hurt in an auto accident and is in a hospital. We'll offer to take the guy to the hospital, get him in our car and haul him up in the country I know, northern Minnesota, until we get the ransom."

Gray interjected: "We'll never bring the guy back, though . . . we'll kill him. That's the safe way. Then he can never identify us."

Clement, in his late 1930s' style wrote: "Seadlund readily agreed to the foul plot for adding murder to kidnapping. A filthy pair of criminal rats were these two—poisonous and slimy creatures on which all America has declared war. Seadlund at last had met a human as low as himself . . ."

The Emily-Spooner Connection

The pair headed north, skirted Seadlund's home community of Ironton and went deep into the wilderness of the north country. At Emily, Minnesota, 40 miles from Ironton, Seadlund brought a quantity of boards in lengths of eight and four feet from the lumberyard. He also purchased two heavy chains with one-inch links and two padlocks. The plan was to build a "nice snug place to hide that ball player."

From the dugout they drove eastward into Wisconsin to the remote village of Spooner. In a spot more remote than the Emily hideout, Seadlund insisted on constructing another dugout. It was

The remote area surrounding Spooner, Wisconsin, where John Henry Seadlund and James Atwood Gray prepared a dugout where they would "jail" a big-name baseball star. When the kidnapping plans fell through, the Spooner dugout site became the grave of a retired Chicago executive Charles S. Ross. Gray also became a victim of Seadlund's terror. *Tom Hollatz photo.*

larger than the first one, seven-feet deep and five-feet wide. The new burial dugout was to be a spare just in case.

It was early August when they left the woods and drifted to more populous Wisconsin summer resort towns. Reading the newspapers, they noted that Dizzy Dean was in a slump for the St. Louis team, and that the Yankees would not play in Chicago for several weeks.

"Dean wouldn't be worth so much dough to the Cards now," Gray said. "Suppose we snatch Ducky Medwick instead. He's a valuable player."

Seadlund quickly pointed out that Medwick was one of the most powerful and aggressive men in either league. Few players would risk physical combat with him on the field. Seadlund feared an attempt to kidnap Medwick would result in nothing more than a good beating for the two of them.

Gray and Seadlund, in quest of a kidnap-for-ransom victim, drifted into Minocqua, Wisconsin. Seadlund scouted a bank there, and was convinced that a robbery would net several thousand dollars, but there were drawbacks.

"There are vigilantes organized around here," Seadlund said. "The citizens have banded together around here to protect rich tourists from stickups. We might get shot before we could get out of town."

They loafed about Minocqua for several days. Gray spent much of his time sipping beer and talking with young men of the town.

After a lackluster kidnapping attempt of Mrs. Olive Borcia, where Seadlund and Gray offered to return her to Chicago for the reduced ransom fee of "only $2,000," the two renewed interest in their original plan—to steal a ball player.

They visited Wrigley Field and watched the Chicago Cubs play on several afternoons, but discovered many obstacles to kidnapping one of the players.

There were several score of uniformed policemen on duty at the park. Dressing rooms for the teams were guarded by a number of officers assigned to keep away overly enthusiastic fans. The players left the park in groups of three and four. The outlaws, Clement wrote, could not think of a subterfuge by which they could approach one of the athletes alone.

With all those obstacles facing them, Seadlund and Gray abandoned their plan to snatch one of the heroes of America's national sport. The risks were too great.

The focus shifted back to the "lots of millionaires" who lived in Illinois.

But first, that bank in Minocqua "is our best bet," Seadlund said. After a visit to Decatur, Illinois, the pair decided to go north to Minocqua. They would head first to Chicago and then on to the small town.

The Hit

It was the evening of Saturday, September 25th, along Wolf Road, just south of the Chicago suburb of Franklin Park, when they spotted a powerful Lincoln sedan.

Driving the car was gray-haired "amiable" Charles S. Ross, 72. Beside him sat his former secretary, Miss Florence Friehage, "a pleasant woman of just past 40."

On the limo was the 1937 Illinois license number 578. The low number, attributed to wealthy and powerful folks, alerted Gray and Seadlund to that possibility.

Ross and Miss Friehage were returning from the Fargo Hotel at Sycamore, Illinois. They had driven to Sycamore for the Fargo's famous steak dinners, or so "True Detective" speculated.

Gray and Seadlund forced Ross to stop the big Lincoln and then forced him into their car. Miss Friehage "watched in horror" and was allowed to go free. The thinking was that Ross, retired owner of the George S. Carrington Company, makers of greeting cards, would be worth at least "250 grand."

Clement, in the magazine article added: "Miss Friehage was a valued friend of both Ross and his wife . . . she remained his secretary . . . on the evening before the kidnapping, she and Mr. Ross had driven to Sycamore for dinner with Mrs. Ross' full knowledge and consent. In fact, Mrs. Ross had planned to accompany them, but had stayed home with a headache at the last moment . . . I want to make it perfectly clear that Florence (Friehage) is one of my best friends . . . there can be absolutely no suspicion that her association with my husband was anything more than a business connection."

The Search

The kidnappers sped northward to Minnesota. Ross was forced to wear glass goggles with wads of cotton in them.

It was late Sunday when they reached their destination near Emily, Minnesota. The two left Ross in the shallow dugout while they went fishing. There Ross would write notes to various friends demanding ransom money. He would ask for $5,000—an amount that would be readily available. Gray and Seadlund always added an extra zero to whatever number Ross scribbled.

After a series of contacts and various assorted ads in the Chicago press, a ransom bundle was delivered near Rockford, Illinois.

Hope that Ross would soon be freed faded quickly.

Caught with a Two-Dollar Bet

On January 14th, the trail of small finds of ransom money would end in California at the Santa Anita race track when John Henry Seadlund stepped up to window No. 51 and placed a two-dollar "show" bet.

Alerted by the G-Men to be on the lookout for ransom bills, Joe Amendt checked the ten-dollar bill placed by one John Henry Seadlund. With the "I'll have to get change" Amendt alerted waiting G-Men.

Seadlund was confronted by G-Men who stated, "I arrest you for the kidnapping of Charles S. Ross."

"It means the chair for me, doesn't it?" Seadlund "managed to whimper."

"True Detective" describes the next scene: " . . . Handcuffs and leg irons were placed on Seadlund. There he sat like some vicious, slimy reptile. He begged for mercy and wept tears of cowardice, but not one word of repentance did he utter. Like others of his vile ilk, he had little sympathy for anyone but himself; none for the victims of his crimes."

The report stated Hoover himself demanded to know where Ross was. "Dead," was the muttered reply. Seadlund informed

HOW G-MEN CAPTURED

SEADLUND

The World's Most Vicious Criminal

BOOK
LENGTH
TRUE
DETECTIVE
FEATURE

BY JOHN
CLEMENT
Special Investigator
for True Detective

John Henry Seadlund. Spread
from "True Detective" magazine.

Hoover that they would find the bodies of Ross and James Atwood
Gray, whom he had murdered too, in a shallow dugout in Spooner,
Wisconsin.

Seadlund explained that he thought Gray was going to kill him
for his share of the ransom. Ross came to his aid. Both, Seadlund
alleged, fought with Gray, who had pulled a pistol. Ross fell into
the dugout. "At the same time I got my hands on Gray's gun and
managed to shoot. Gray fell into the hole on top of Ross and wounded
him."

Seadlund claimed to have attempted to save Ross, but that the aged man seemed to be dying from injuries suffered in the fall. "I thought the best thing to do would be to put him out of his misery," the arch-criminal calmly related.

On the afternoon of January 21, the bodies of Ross and Gray were removed from the Spooner dugout. The remaining $30,000 ransom was recovered the following day near Emily. Seadlund had buried it beside a railroad post and fired four shots into the sign to mark the place.

Late in the afternoon of March 16th, the jury (in some 30 minutes) said Seadlund must die in the electric chair on April 16th in the Cook County jail.

Early in the morning of July 14th, two hours after he arranged his own funeral with a Minnesota undertaker, John Henry Seadlund, the "back woods boy who wanted to be a big shot in the underworld," was lifted lifeless from Cook County's electric chair.

OTHER MOBSTERS

Joe "Polock Joe" Saltis

Joe Saltis made a fortune running beer on the South Side of Chicago and Wausau, Wisconsin, during the bullet-riddled Prohibition era. John Kobler in *Capone: The Life and World of Al Capone* makes mention of the man:

> On the the Southwest Side, [was] the Saltis-McErlane gang. Joe Saltis was a hulking, slow-witted Pole, a saloonkeeper, so enriched by Prohibition that he bought a summer estate in Wisconsin's Eagle River Country, the playground of millionaire sportsmen. If opposed in his efforts to enlarge his speakeasy holdings, he used primitive methods of persuasion. When a woman who owned an ice-cream parlor refused to convert it into a speakeasy under his control, he clubbed her to death . . .

It had been one of Saltis' dreams to live in the Northwoods of Wisconsin and he did purchase an estate on 238-acre Barker Lake, a widening of the east fork of the Chippewa River, some eight miles north of Winter, Wisconsin. He surrounded his main lodge with several guest cabins where visiting "firemen" or "blazers" (gunmen) could relax away from the heat (not just temperature) of Chicago. (The estate now is a resort, with dining room, cabins and a golf course.)

Saltis, used to having things go his way in Chicago, was apt, even

Photos courtesy the FBI.

Joe 'Polack Joe' Saltis, beer baron of the southwest side of Chicago. *FBI photo.*

Bootlegger Roger "The Terrible" Touhy's police mug shot. *Photo courtesty Jay Robert Nash.*

in the Northwoods, to enjoy himself as he pleased. One of the pleasures he afforded himself was to fish at the Winter, Wisconsin, dam. The river below the dam was alive with fish, supposedly protected by law, but its waters had been violated more and more frequently by Saltis. Game Warden Ernest Swift of Hayward decided to put a stop to it.

With augmented forces that August day in 1930, Ernest Swift planned the arrest. As his men stalked along the river banks they managed to slip past the guards Saltis had posted to prevent his being disturbed. They were able to reach Saltis and leveled their rifles at him.

"What's the idea of all the artillery?" Saltis said, eyeing the guns.

"I understand you want to shoot it out with me," answered Swift, "so here I am."

The Saltis guards moved in, but their chief offered no resistance. He was led off to court and fined $50 for fishing within 100 feet of the dam. Two companions, Ed Morrison and Joe Sedovich of Chicago were fined $25 each.

Roger "The Terrible" Touhy

Roger "The Terrible" Touhy was a powerful bootlegging king of the Chicago area. His hold was so complete and backed with such firepower, that it was said to be unchallengeable. He also manufactured a superior beer, and his kegs—made at his own cooperage—were leak proof. He also limited his illegal activities, and was cheered by his Des Plaines neighbors for keeping brothels out of town.

When "The Terrible" vacationed, it was often in Minocqua, Wisconsin, a quaint, beautiful town known as the "Island City." Jim Ford, now of Green Bay, Wisconsin, remembers his highly unusual fishing method.

> Touhy stood up [in the boat] one day when they were out fishing and unloaded [his tommygun] on the waters. That old machine gun blasted away. It was good for a laugh. And if I remember, he did get a fish or two . . .

It should be remembered that in the 1930s, it was legal to fish with a pistol at your side. This was a practice observed by many of the fishing guides. The gun was used to put a bullet in the head of a fighting musky after it was caught and pulled alongside the boat. The guns—usually .32s—were abolished when the practice got out of hand, including putting holes in the bottom of boats, several self-inflicted injuries, and even the occasional shot fired at other boats that encroached on favorite fishing spots. Nowadays a club is used to subdue the musky, because, guns or no, a 25-pound musky with shark-like teeth bouncing around on the bottom of a boat with a big treble hook sticking half out of its mouth is still a dangerous thing.

Frank Nitti

"Yeah, I remember Frank Nitti," said Jim Ford. "He vacationed in the Northwoods, too."

Nitti was a Capone mob lieutenant, but his importance in Big Al's gang may have been exaggerated. He seemed to have played a larger role in his portrayal on the television show "The Untouchables."

Nitti, it was alleged, was to be Big Al's replacement if and when he was sent to prison. Yet when the national crime mob was being established in the early 1930's, its founders dealt with Paul "The Waiter" Ricca as the head of Chicago's Capone mob. Nitti wasn't even told about the maneuver. On March 19, 1943, the day after a verbal fight with Ricca, Nitti walked along some railroad tracks, drew his pistol and killed himself.

Is Jimmy Hoffa Buried in the Northwoods?

When former feisty Teamster official Jimmy Hoffa disappeared, serious thought was given to the theory that he may have been entombed somewhere in the vast forests of the Northwoods. Hoffa had often visited the Northwoods, thus sparking the inquiry.

That Northwoods connection included a link to the late Allen M. Dorfman, Hoffa's close associate. Dorfman owned the Jack O'Lantern Lodge at Eagle River, Wisconsin, a community noted for its savage muskies and the largest inland chain of lakes in the world (29 lakes). The Jack O'Lantern was a well-known retreat for Teamsters officials and Dorfman's friends and business associates, including Hoffa.

When Hoffa disappeared, a search was made in the woods near the Jack O'Lantern. Nothing was found, but that didn't mean Hoffa wasn't buried in the woods. There are thousands of acres in the surrounding Northern Highland State Forest, the Nicolet Forest, and the American Legion State Forest.

Sam "Golf Bag" Hunt

"I often drove Sam 'Golf Bag' Hunt everywhere he wanted to go in Minocqua," said Jim Ford, ". . . including to and from Ma

Frank Nitti. *Photo courtesy the Bureau of Alcohol, Tobacco and Firearms.*

Bailey's." (Ma Bailey's was one of the better brothels of the North-woods. It is now known as Joe Kelly's Landing.)

Sam Hunt was considered the toughest of the Capone mob enforcers along with Machine Gun McGurn. They were the "blazers," and Hunt was credited with killing no less than twenty men. He got the name "Golf Bag" because he had the habit of going on murder errands with a golf bag that held a sawed-off shotgun. Chicago police once arrested him and brought him before the famed gangster-era Judge John H. Lyle. In Judge Lyle's book, *The Dry and Lawless Years*, he wrote of Sam Hunt coming before him:

> He asserted straight-faced that he was carrying the gun in the bag because he was going duck hunting. Before we could pursue this interesting combination of sports, his attorney requested a change of venue which I had to grant.

It may seem ironic, but on that particular occasion before Judge Lyle, Hunt may have been going duck hunting in the Northwoods.

Jack Zuta

Zuta's escape to the peace and quiet of Wisconsin was tied directly with the murder of a Chicago *Tribune* reporter, Alfred "Jake" Lingle on June 9, 1930.

Lingle was bound for the Illinois Central station just south of Tribune Tower where he planned to take the 1:30 train for the Washington Park race track in Homewood.

Lingle entered the tunnel to the IC trains when he was gunned down by a bullet to his brain. He never knew what hit him. His cigar was still clenched in his teeth when his body hit the floor. His fingers still clutched the racing form.

It was Zuta who reportedly fingered the hit as the work of the Capone gang. Big Al, who always arranged to be out of town when a hit was going down, reportedly had hired Leo Brothers, a gangster from St. Louis, to end the mob's ties to Lingle.

Zuta knew he was a marked man; Capone knew he wasn't saying nice things about him and would want his termination.

It was then, in August of 1930, that Jack Zuta registered under the name of J.H. Goodman of Aurora, Illinois, at the Lakeview Hotel on the west shore of Waukesha County's Upper Nemahbin Lake. It was August 1st. The strains of a music box drifted through an open window of the quiet resort. Inside on a dance floor, several couples were dancing.

Zuta, a short and swarthy man, stood next to the music box, feeding it nickels.

Outside, two automobiles drove up to the resort. No one noticed this because a main highway wound past the resort along the shore of the lake. Many cars passed.

Two gentlemen entered and spotted Zuta, who had dropped another nickel into the music box. As Zuta turned, a bullet crashed into his mouth. He tried to escape. More lead struck his head and body. He never spoke as he sagged to the floor. Two gunmen walked to his side and fired several more times into his lifeless body.

Brothers, who probably got $500 for the hit, was convicted of the slaying of Alfred Lingle and served nine years in prison for it, dying of a heart attack soon after his release.

Mafia Princess in the Northwoods

Antoinette "Toni" Giancana, in her book *Mafia Princess—Growing Up in Sam Giancana's Family* (William Morrow and Company, Inc.) recalled her family's vacation in the Northwoods of Wisconsin:

> . . . I was a little more than four years old when Sam decided the family needed a vacation in Rhinelander, Wisconsin. Though my memories of that time are somewhat fuzzy, pictures from family albums and recollections of close relatives project an image of Sam as a handsome, slim, street-wise hustler with a full head of hair, carefully tailored clothes and a flashy car . . .
>
> When we went to Rhinelander, no expense was spared. We stayed at a luxurious hotel, where we had a suite of rooms, including separate bedrooms for Momma and Dad and for Bonnie and me, together with separate baths and a sitting/living room complete with a fully-stocked bar.
>
> It turned out to be a wonderful time, with Sam and Momma taking me shopping, swimming together at an almost private beach, and picnicking, something I had never done before. It was a happy time and I did my damnedest to please . . .

Sam Giancana or "Momo" as the mobsters called him, was chief of Chicago's Mafia who smoked Cuban cigars, drove a pink Cadillac, and talked out of the side of his mouth.

He was a short balding man with a sixth-grade education and was the successor to Al Capone. He was a top member, too, of Cosa Nostra, the national crime syndicate. He controlled the protection rackets, pinball machines, prostitution, numbers games, narcotics, loan sharks, extortioners, counterfeiters and bookmakers in the Chicago area.

The quiet peace of a Northwoods river near Rhinelander, Wisconsin. It was here that Antoinette Giancana, daughter of mobster Sam Giancana, and her family acted like a real family for the first time, away from federal surveillance. After reading Toni's book *Mafia Princess"* I wrote and asked her where in Rhinelander it was that they vacationed. Sadly, she didn't remember the name of the resort. *Tom Hollatz photo.*

THEY REMEMBER

Jim Ford Remembers

One who knew the Prohibition days in the Northwoods was Jim Ford, the "Durkee Spice King." Ford played on the Minocqua, Wisconsin, town baseball team in 1938 and was a standout at second base and shortstop. He played in the Boston Red Sox organization and, later, was a scout for the Pittsburgh Pirates. But in the 1930s, he would pick up extra money driving the gangsters around the Northwoods.

When I played baseball in Minocqua, there was a place near the fish hatchery in Woodruff called Ma Bailey's. Charlie Koch of the Belle Isle would tell me some of the guys in his saloon wanted to go out there, so I'd drive them out. I'd sit at the bar at Ma Bailey's, and these guys would head to the back rooms with the girls.

Here I was 19 years old, just sitting there. Some of the girls would come down to the end of the bar and talk with me. I did these driving errands weekly and got to know the gals.

The funny thing is those girls would come into town on Sunday afternoon to watch me play baseball. Every time I'd get up to bat, they'd honk their horns. The local citizens didn't like it when the prostitutes cheered for me. They wondered what was going on.

I remember when Charlie Koch, owner of the Belle Isle in Minocqua asked me to drive some friends to a hotel in Winchester.

I knew they were gangsters, but I didn't know their names. When

Jim Ford of Green Bay, Wisconsin, known as the Durkee Spice King, played with the Minocqua town baseball team in the late 1930s. For money, the young Ford did favors for the gangsters, including driving them to Ma Bailey's whorehouse in nearby Woodruff. Ma Bailey's is now an excellent restaurant called Joe Kelly's Landing. *Photo Camera/100 Collection.*

The Belle Isle in Minocqua, Wisconsin, was a popular tourist attraction during the 1930s. One of its features was a direct wire to Arlington Park Race Track. Now called the Landmark, the saloon is the anchor of the downtown business community on Highway 51. *Tom Hollatz photo.*

I dropped them off at the hotel, I helped them with their bags. That's when I spotted their sawed-off shotguns and a Thompson submachine gun. Everything went good. No problems.

Then on the way back to Minocqua, we stopped to pick up some hitchhiking girls. They didn't know it, but they were in for the ride of their lives.

We were [driving] with the windows down as we headed south on Highway 51. Suddenly they popped their weapons through the windows and started blasting away . . . at those glass resistors on the telephone poles. It was target practice time. I never saw two more frightened girls . . ."

I wish I could remember the kid's name. It was about 1929 when Ralph and Al Capone were known far and wide. A twelve-year-old boy in Cleveland read all about Ralph in the newspapers. He traveled all the way from Cleveland to Chicago, and then to Cicero to meet Ralph. The bodyguards were baffled, but they took him to Ralph. Ralph was amused and very kind to the lad. He took the young man to dinner and then to the theater. He also put him up overnight, and then sent him back to Cleveland.

One thing I've always wondered is why Emil Wanatka Sr. was never questioned. I always wondered why Dillinger came up here. I heard from some of the guys I played baseball with that Emil came from Racine. He was a waiter in the Bohemia Club there and made a lot of contacts in Chicago. Then he moved to Chicago, became a bartender, and finally owned his own place. When Emil moved to the Northwoods, those contacts knew the north was a nice safe place.

I heard from Homer Van Meter's girlfriend, Marie Conforti. [After the escape from Little Bohemia] Dillinger, Van Meter and a third man—can't remember his name—left Manitowish Waters and headed for Wausau. The call from the police was to look for three men in a car. They wound up north of Wausaw. Two men got out and took the street car to the south end of town [while the third drove the car]. There they got back into the car. They drove off Highway 51 to take Highway 29 to St. Paul. That's what Marie told me . . .

Jim Snyder

Jim Snyder, a Minocqua realtor and a teacher, recalled the Northwoods in the early 1940s. Snyder sold newspapers in Minocqua at the time. "Many times I was stopped by a Chicago gangster— 'Hey, kid, got a scratch sheet?'" Snyder also recalled going to the Belle Isle and other Minocqua saloons to hear the live racing action over the direct line from the Belle Isle to Arlington Park Race Track.

Virgil Wrege

Virgil Wrege, a masonry contractor from Lac du Flambeau, Wisconsin, said he knew Capone's bodyguard:

He was 90 pounds soaking wet. He was dying of cancer, always in pain. I would meet him at the old Log Cabin saloon on Highway 47. He would drink a pint of whiskey to kill the pain—every night. He was always with a woman. The mob paid her to take care of him— just so he wouldn't spill the beans. One thing about Skinny Mazurka I'll never forget. He knocked off many hoods in his day without batting an eye. Yet, he was afraid of dying.

Frank Nitti? Yes, I knew him. I did him a lot of favors, driving now and then to buy him booze. He always paid me well—$4.00 an hour. And every time I bought booze, say it was four bottles, he'd pay me for eight. He was generous.

Albert Cobe, in his 80s, of Lac du Flambeau, Wisconsin. Cobe talked with Ole Catfish after he was forced to house and feed Baby Face Nelson after his escape from Little Bohemia. *Tom Hollatz photo.*

Albert Cobe

Albert Cobe, who admits to being in his 80s, is the "gentleman scholar" of Lac du Flambeau. He's a most fascinating character. Once a college math teacher and a great local basketball player, he was also a former pro golfer. He remembered Ole "Catfish" Johnson who hosted George "Baby Face" Nelson in his rustic Lac du Flambeau home after Nelson escaped the Feds at Little Bohemia.

Albert once asked Catfish if Baby Face had paid him for his stay of some three days. "Ole said no, but then I started to smile. He was wearing a new hat and some new shoes. We all knew . . ."

William Yeschek

William Yeschek, prominent Minocqua realtor and attorney, recalled those Dillinger days in the Northwoods. His family operated the famed Crawling Stone Resort in Lac du Flambeau.

I remember Roy Kneiszel. He was part of the search team after

Opposite: A great blue heron slips gently across a Northwoods lake. "Simple pleasures . . . are the last refuge of the complex." So said Oscar Wilde. *Tom Hollatz photo.*

Dillinger and Baby Face escaped. He worked for us. Well, he went out in this massive hunt, with a gun. He was called on to block roads on Highway 70. When he returned, he checked his gun and found out it didn't have a firing pin. He could have died . . .

Richard Timmons

The publisher of the Rhinelander *Daily News*, Richard Timmons, told about a local merchant who, in the Dillinger days of 1934, outfitted some well-dressed "hood types."

This giant big black car pulls [up] in front and they all get out. They're well dressed, mind. They enter the store and pull down the shades. They demand to get new suits and now, complete with tailoring. The way Murley [the store owner] tells it, they then paid with cash in brown bags. He also noted that they were wearing guns, and he joked with them. "Should I measure around the gun belts?" I would.

Louis St. Germaine

Louis St. Germaine, known as "Louis No. 1," was one of the best fishing guides in the Northwoods. His clients were a "Who's who" in the celebrity world, including Bing Crosby and Al Capone. One day while guiding "two notorious" gangsters on White Sand Lake in Lac du Flambeau, Wisconsin, he had an unusual experience. It was time for one of his fabled Northwoods' shore lunches. While Louis prepared his mouth-watering walleye fillets, the two hoods decided to mix martinis in the minnow bucket—just for laughs. The lead from the walls of the pail corrupted the concoction. The two gangsters took sick. Louis, who did not drink booze, rushed them to the local hospital where their stomachs were pumped.

Donald Rasmussen

Donald Rasmussen of Wausau, Wisconsin, remembers Mercer in the days of Ralph Capone. He worked on the C&NW railroad for 40 years, working in Mercer, Ironwood, Hurley and many other stations. He said he relieved the agent in Hurley once.

I lived in a rooming house and ate at Connie's so I became sort of a resident of Hurley.

Our truck went out of Hurley south to Mercer and beyond. It cut across the Montreal River which separates Wisconsin from Michigan and Hurley from Ironwood. It made a big curve and on a roadbed which was built high enough to where it was almost as high as a two-story building. Riding in an engine you could look into these second-story rooms and, once in a while, see the young ladies plying their trade . . . before World War II the conditions in Hurley were a lot dif-

Louis St. Germaine, known as "Louis No. 1," was one of the best fishing guides in the Northwoods. Gangsters were some of his clients on fishing trips. *Photo Courtesy of Dillman's Sand Lake Resort.*

ferent. The old Hurley Hotel burned down and many of the bright lights are now missing . . . so are other famous buildings.

During the early days . . . whiskey was shipped into Hurley in big barrels [55 gallon drums] and would be stored in a locked room separate from the regular warehouse or freight house. No doubt this was to prevent pilferage. Some gents learned about this room . . . the bottom of the room was made of thick bridge timbers . . . they crawled under the room and drilled holes through the floor, hitting the barrels and filling pails with whiskey. When the pails were filled, they'd leave and let the barrel [run] until it was dry . . . later a boiler plate was placed on the floor.

The Author

Tom Hollatz adjacent to his "Electrolux" word processor in his home overlooking Trout Lake in Boulder Junction, Wisconsin, "The Musky Capital of the World." His only heirloom (over his right shoulder) is a Dick Tracy cartoon given to him by his late friend Chester Gould, Tracy's creator. Hollatz received the cartoon in 1972. At the time, Tracy sported a mustache. Hollatz is the author of several books, including *The Loon Book* and *The White Earth Snowshoe Guide Book* also published by North Star Press of St. Cloud. *Photo by Porter Dean.*

Bibliography

The author wishes to acknowledge his indebtedness to the authors and editors of the following books and periodicals consulted for reference.

Helmer, William J. *The Gun that Made the Twenties Roar*. The Gun Room Press, 1969.

Kobler, John. *Capone: The Life and World of Al Capone*. Fawcett Crest Books, 1971.

Lyle, John H. *The Dry and Lawless Years*. Prentice-Hall, Inc., 1960.

Moore, Todd. *Dillinger: Dillinger Faces*. Kangaroo Court Publishing, 1987.

Murray, George. *The Legacy of Al Capone*. G. P. Putnam's Sons, 1975.

Nash, Jay Robert. *Bloodletters and Bad Men*. Warner Books, 1973.

Nash, Jay Robert. *Murder Among the Rich and Famous*. Arlington House, 1983.

Nash, Jay Robert. *Almanac of World Crime*. Bonanza Books, 1981.

Nash, Jay Robert. *The Dillinger Dossier*. December Press, 1970.

Reilly, Bill. *Big Al's Official Guide to Chicago-ese*. Contemporary Books, Inc. 1982.

Sifakis, Carl. *The Encyclopedia of American Crime.* Facts on File, Inc., 1982.

Toland, John. *The Dillinger Days.* Random House, 1963.

Wallechinsky, David and Wallace, Irving. *The People's Almanac No. 2.* William Morrow and Company, Inc., 1978.

Author unknown. *Life of Al Capone in Pictures and Chicago's Gang Wars.* Lake Michigan Publishing Company, 1931.

The Chicago *Tribune.*
The Chicago *Sun Times.*
The Duluth *News-Tribune.*
The Green Bay *Press-Gazette.*
The Lakeland *Times.*
The Milwaukee *Journal.*
The Racine *Times.*
The Vilas County *News-Review.*